dark horse

HOW CHALLENGER COMPANIES
RISE TO PROMINENCE

DAN MACK

SAKURA PUBLISHING
Hermitage, Pennsylvania
USA

dark horse

HOW CHALLENGER COMPANIES
RISE TO PROMINENCE

DAN MACK

DARK HORSE: HOW CHALLENGER COMPANIES RISE TO PROMINENCE
Copyright © 2013 by Dan Mack

SAKURA PUBLISHING
PO BOX 1681
HERMITAGE, PA 16148
WWW.SAKURA -PUBLISHING.COM

Ordering Information:
Quantity sales. Special discounts are available on quantity purchases by corporations, associations, and others. For details, contact the publisher at the address above. Orders by U.S. trade bookstores and wholesalers. Please contact Sakura Publishing: Tel: (330) 360-5131; or visit www.sakura-publishing.com.

Book Cover and Interior Design by Rania Meng
Edited by Peter Santilli
First Edition Printed in the United States of America

ISBN-10: 0988962861
ISBN-13: 978-0-9889628-6-6
14 13 12 11 10 / 10 9 8 7 6 5 4 3 2 1

DEDICATIONS

This book is dedicated to a group of inspirational dark horse companies and leaders who demonstrated to me that size is only a state of mind, and that unleashing one's identity can transform anything.

To Rich Swanson, Ric Durr, Wayne Bennett, Heather Angus-Lee, Evan Mack, Noah Mack and the members of the Elevation Forum for serving as incredible industry influencers, friends, and advisors on this project.

To my wife, Michele for your patience and love.

And to Abba for your grace.

table of contents

People want to be part of something larger than themselves. They want to be part of something they're really proud of, that they'll fight for, sacrifice for, and trust.

—HOWARD SCHULTZ, STARBUCKS

Introduction:
WHAT IS A "DARK HORSE" ANYWAY?

All growth is a leap in the dark, a spontaneous unpremeditated act without benefit of experience.

—HENRY MILLER, AUTHOR

Everyone loves a dark horse—the come-from-behind winner that no one expects. We cheer for them, marvel at their tenacity, and hope for their victory over stronger, better-known competitors.

But *why* do dark horses win? They aren't favored to win, and often for good reason. They usually don't have big money invested in them; they have no history of winning, and not many people have heard of them. The usual formula for winning the race just isn't there.

Yet they win anyway.

A little history of the term "dark horse" reveals the effects of this stunning and disruptive phenomenon. The first instance of the phrase "dark horse" was in Benjamin Disraeli's 1831 novel *The Young Duke* in a scene about a horse race:

"The first favorite was never heard of, the second favorite was never seen after the distance post … and a *dark horse*, which had never been thought of … rushed past the grandstand in sweeping triumph. The spectators were almost too surprised to cheer."

Bigger, better-known competitors often don't pay any or enough attention to dark horses until it's too late and the dark horses streak past. Surprise is indeed the reaction of spectators—competitors, their investors, and the marketplace at large—when dark horses win. The sound of no one cheering (at first) is the silence of dropped jaws and boardrooms hushed by surprise.

This book is my way of taking some of the mystique out of how dark horses win. But not all of the mystique: some success factors are intangible. And besides, who doesn't like a little surprise?

This book is also documentation of all I have learned over twenty-five years as a leader of two dark horse organizations, and the insights gathered during numerous strategy and consulting engagements with a wide variety of smaller, winning organizations. I have personally researched, interviewed, or consulted with well over a hundred emerging companies that, by all accounts, were outmatched by competition—yet they were winning. Not only that, these dark horse companies seemed to be having more fun during the trip towards the finish line than the larger companies they competed against!

MY FIRST TASTE OF BEING A DARK HORSE

My interest in understanding *why* dark horse companies are successful goes back to my own journey of helping to launch a little upstart consumer brand called PURELL in 1997. I joined GOJO Industries as the head of their sales and customer marketing team during the first year of the national launch and roll-out of PURELL Instant Hand Sanitizer.

This new invention, which had one-hundred-percent share of the category, was being attacked by some of the best consumer product companies in the world: Soft Soap, Suave, Dial, and Lysol. These juggernauts began crowding out our brand; our market share was in a free fall. We quickly realized that our PURELL brand was vulnerable, despite the fanfare, awards, and recognition we had received upon launch. Our very jobs were on the line.

That was my first up-close-and-personal experience of what it feels like to be a dark horse. Since the big boys had entered the game, everyone in the industry thought our PURELL party was over. In fact, one old friend walked up to me at an industry function, gave me a hug and said, "It was still a good ride, right?"

Being hundreds of times smaller than the mega-multinationals we competed against, we didn't have the industry relationships and deep pockets they had. So we fell back substantially in the race, losing some three-quarters of our market share.

But GOJO Industries was a fifty-year-old company with deep formulation insight; it was passionate about the consumer, thrived in competition, was very agile, and it understood hand hygiene better than any company in the world. And, oh yeah, they believed in the vision of the brand and had designed a thoughtful blueprint for success. They saw the finish line, and created a culture which would allow them to win.

You see, GOJO had been making and selling soap and hand sanitizer dispensers to hospitals, businesses, restaurant restrooms, health clubs, and government facilities across the U.S. for many years; the PURELL consumer launch was just an extension of their identity. (We'll talk a lot about corporate identity in the next chapter). So when the going got tough, GOJO and PURELL were up for the fight. The PURELL brand carried a 75 percent market share prior to being sold to Pfizer Consumer Healthcare. Even in the smallest of categories this level of market dominance doesn't occur too often!

BLIND SPOTS

Why do you think the TV show *Shark Tank* is so popular? You would think that a show about a bunch of finely dressed business people assessing new business ventures is more fodder for boardrooms than family living rooms. So what's the hook?

The show's creators are harnessing the dark horse phenomenon. People tune in to witness what unknown people with few resources and fewer connections can accomplish with great ideas, strategy, passion, and a strong sense of identity and purpose. The dark horses are the candidates who stand in front of the rich investors with all these elements in place. They're the ones who persuade the sharks to invest in their products, regardless of their blind spots and odds stacked against them.

All of us have blind spots that limit our success and are often stumbling blocks to growth. Over a three-year period I sat down with and interviewed the top retail executives from many of the largest retailers in the country.

The insights uncovered were telling and helped me understand how dark horse companies can sneak up on their larger competitors. It is very clear that many organizations, big and small, are not as aligned and valuable as they may think they are. In fact, their blind spots are killing them, and they don't even know it.

What we found is that the most vibrant and healthy dark horse organizations work diligently to increase their own corporate awareness, shining a light on areas that could hinder their future success. The best organizations want to know how they are doing and create an atmosphere where their customers, employees, suppliers and partners share the naked truth. A big part of their success is that their leadership is open to criticism, which allows them to stay in reality. They operate in a culture of stark raving honesty.

Conversely, many organizations struggle with a number of blind spots that often impede growth including:

1. NOT UNDERSTANDING THE MOST VITAL PERSONAL PRIORITIES OF CUSTOMERS
2. NOT BEING PERCEIVED AS DIFFERENT FROM THE COMPETITION
3. NOT BRINGING THE MOST RELEVANT ASSETS, KNOWLEDGE, AND/OR IDEAS TO THE CUSTOMER
4. NOT LISTENING OR READING BETWEEN THE LINES OF WHAT CUSTOMERS ARE SAYING/THINKING/FEELING

IT'S ALWAYS PERSONAL

Winning organizations know that business is not transactional: it's personal. They set their own rules of engagement, and their corporate values are shared by everyone across the organization. Expectations are clear; employees are encouraged to find and use new resources. Fear of failure is discouraged, and power is shared. Sound too utopian?

We have also found that some of the best companies are also somewhat *messy* at times. Even though they have clearly defined the box they play in, they are always evaluating, innovating, and tinkering around the edges of their business. This flexible, curious, and agile culture provides stimulation for lots of innovation and ideas. Nothing is perfect, and they like it that way.

Speed-to-market is another characteristic of successful dark horses. As one customer shared with me, "The best companies move from prototype to end product quicker than competitors, and have learned to deal with the messiness." Winning companies are constantly in the process of re-invigorating their business, leaving competitors in their wake. They ask a lot of questions and never assume they are done understanding the industry or their business.

Dark horse organizations are also good at flying under the radar. This can give them an advantage in sneaking up on the competition, but can also result in them being marginalized or flat-out ignored. However, the stronger its sense of purpose, the more likely a dark horse organization will leave its imprint on the business landscape. They can even go so far as to become the catalysts for dramatic innovation and sometimes even larger societal or cultural shifts. We have recently seen this with the Google and Apple revolutions.

Whether you lead a small business, a consulting practice, a sports team, or a not-for-profit enterprise, this book will reveal the clues left behind by winning organizations. The best leaders and companies bring more than unique products or services to the market; they consistently tap into the ten growth enablers outlined in this book including:

» THEIR BUSINESS IS PERSONAL; IT'S AN EXTENSION OF THEIR IDENTITY, AND IT'S ABOUT MORE THAN PROFIT.
» THEY LISTEN WELL AND STAY IN ALIGNMENT WITH TOP CUSTOMERS.
» THEY USE THEIR ORGANIZATION'S HIDDEN ASSETS TO CREATE DIFFERENTIATING VALUE.
» THEY CREATE A CLEAR, VIBRANT BUSINESS BLUEPRINT AND SHARE IT OPENLY WITH EMPLOYEES.
» THEY CAREFULLY AND WISELY PICK THEIR CUSTOMERS AND THEIR PARTNERS.
» THEY CO-CREATE INNOVATION WITH CUSTOMERS.
» THEY MOVE QUICKLY TO MEET CONSUMER SHIFTS TO CREATE NEW EXPERIENCES.
» THEY INFLUENCE THE INFLUENCERS WHO HELP BUILD THEIR BRAND.
» THEY ARE VERY AGILE AND NIMBLE, AND SEIZE NEW OPPORTUNITIES MUCH FASTER THAN COMPETITORS.
» CORPORATE CULTURE OPERATES WITH A SPIRIT OF GRACE AND HONOR.

This book is divided into ten chapters (or ideas) that describe practices and philosophies held by many dark horse companies that have successfully differentiated them from their competitors. Within each chapter I share with you companies that truly exemplify the practice outlined in the chapter. I've also included a set of provocative questions called Thought Starters at the end of each chapter. Consider bringing a Thought Starter topic to a staff meeting at *your* dark horse company to kick-start a conversation that can transform your team!

I sincerely hope that during and after reading this book you will take the time to reflect on and to question your own corporate culture, your leadership style, and your strategies for engaging customers.

Enjoy these stories, think about the ideas, let them marinate, and then *act decisively*.

Chapter 1:

IDENTITY

(It's Personal)

To be nobody but yourself in a world which is doing its best, night and day, to make you like everybody else means to fight the hardest battle which any human being can fight; and never stop fighting.

—E.E. CUMMINGS, POET

I have always been intrigued by the idea of a dark horse, and in many ways, I believe we are all dark horses to one degree or another. My own story can attest to this. As a young boy, I struggled to overcome a debilitating stuttering problem; later in life, it was my fear of public speaking and the effects of my father's alcoholism that I had to overcome. I might have started a bit behind the pack, but in moving forward, I fought and won battles that were truly my own. Dealing with personal hardships helped forge the person I am today; such is the story of many dark horses.

It was also some help, as I was growing in the business world, to hear the following sage advice from an unlikely source:

"You do not merely want to be considered just the best of the best. You want to be considered the only ones who do what you do." That is not the idea of a business school professor, but the vision of former Grateful Dead front man and founder, Jerry Garcia. Garcia was a visionary who understood brand identity better than many of the top companies celebrated today. His millions of followers, zealots, and brand evangelists were drawn by his authenticity, not his marketing campaign. The Grateful Dead never earned mass appeal, never littered the charts with hits, but to this day, they may arguably have the truest

» *Why is it that **over forty percent** of the companies that were at the top of the Fortune 500 in 2000 were no longer there in 2010?*

» *Why is it that the **majority of new product launches fail**, never making it to the shelf, let alone make it into the consumer's shopping basket?*

brand and *brand identity* to ever have hit the stage. This is a lesson for business, brand marketers, and leaders of all types.

When it comes to brand success, an organization with size, relationships, and momentum has an enormous advantage in building successful new brands. The next time you do your grocery shopping, visit the health and beauty department and look at how few companies dominate the majority of the allocated shelf space in the department. Large multinationals such as Procter & Gamble, Unilever, Novartis, Pfizer, Johnson & Johnson, Revlon and L'Oréal control the majority of the shelves in most drugstores across the country. No wonder it is difficult for a smaller organization to survive, let alone flourish, among these giants.

Colgate and Procter & Gamble's Crest control well over 60 percent of the oral-health section sale in most retailers.

Now, as a case in point, if you take a look at the broader oral category, the shelf is controlled by five large branded companies including Proctor & Gamble, Colgate, Johnson & Johnson, GlaxoSmithKline, and Church & Dwight. P&G's *ocean of blue* packaging includes Crest, Scope mouthwash, Glide dental floss, and Oral-B toothbrushes. Colgate's *sea of red* also grabs your eye with a strong complement of items such as Colgate toothpaste and toothbrushes, Wisp mini toothbrushes, and their specialty mouthwashes and kids' toothpastes.

If you take a closer look, you'll notice that Johnson & Johnson's Listerine mouthwash, GlaxoSmithKline's Sensodyne and Aquafresh toothpastes, and Church & Dwight's Arm & Hammer toothpastes and toothbrushes round out the set. A limited number of companies control the majority of choices in a category that almost every consumer must purchase at some time during the year.

The big and powerful may control the shelf, but there is always room for challengers.

As you continue your walk down the aisle, you will notice a number of much smaller, highly differentiated brands. Many times these challenger brands appeal to smaller groups of zealous consumers who are often very loyal, passionate and emotionally connected to the brand.

Let's return to our oral care category example. Brands such as Dentek, GUM, TheraBreath and Stim-U-Dent may not be large, but they are distinct and have created a unique identity.

Dark horse brands are on the shelves in all product categories. So how does a dark horse company make it to the shelf in a market dominated by big brands?

Now more than ever, having the most resources and a cupboard of compelling assets alone guarantees nothing. Today, it is *identity* accompanied by *imagination* that sets the table for sustainable success. What's *inside* —as well as outside —really does matter.

Size matters, but identity matters even more.

WHO DO YOU INTEND TO BE?

In his introspective book *Leadership is an Art*, Max De Pree (former CEO of Herman Miller Inc.) conveys his leadership identity with one question. It's not "What are our profit goals? What is our market share?" or even "What is our long term business plan?" Instead, he asks his organization, "Who do we intend to be?"[1] How you answer the "who" question provides valuable insight into your organization's likelihood for success. Business success has as much to do with a company's calling and identity as the ideas packed within their four walls.

Herman Miller is consistently recognized as one of Fortune Magazine's Most Admired Companies, leading with innovation, product design, sustainability, and leadership development over the last two decades. Their identity—not their leadership control—guides their corporate culture.

Most people desperately want to pull themselves and their organizations back to safety, equilibrium, and order. However, real innovation is born when everyone is pressed to a place of disorder or to a position of trying to hold on. It is operating on the edge where innovation's best chances lie. Bruce Springsteen got it right when he stated, "We are at best when we are barely holding on."[2]

Real sustainable value is a byproduct of the creative tension that only the bravest, healthiest leaders allow to occur.

To create something special means you must be able to trust people around you, but most companies are not able or willing to deal with the ambiguity, turmoil, and risk of failure that accompanies the process of letting go and trusting. Most organizations major in being in control, putting up boundaries, and renting souls to work for them. But dark horse companies have found that controlling behavior never unlocks

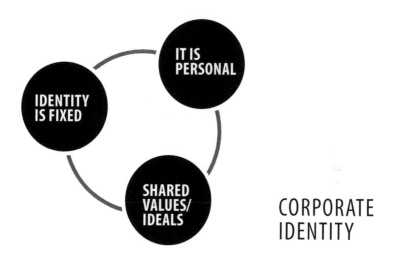

CORPORATE IDENTITY

peak performance, nor does it attract and retain good leaders. A dark horse understands that business strategy works best when it is fueled by a larger purpose that transcends the profit sheet and is grounded in a business model which unleashes their identity. They don't practice leadership control; rather, they allow their identity to shape the marketplace.

The cultures of the top emerging companies we have studied are governed by three drivers:

» THEIR CORPORATE IDENTITY IS FIXED, AND THEIR BUSINESS IS AN EXPRESSION OF THEIR IDENTITY.
» THEIR BUSINESS IS VERY PERSONAL, PURPOSEFUL, AND IT RUNS DEEP.
» THEY HAVE CREATED CLARITY OF VISION, AND EVERYONE CHOOSES TO OPERATE WITH SHARED VALUES AND IDEALS.

FIXED IDENTITY

It is difficult to honestly look in the mirror and wrestle with who you *are*, who you are *not*, and who you hope to become. I discovered this personally when, shortly after graduating from college, I attended a leadership training conference. One exercise I had to endure was to be filmed as I spoke before my peers, who were later tasked with critiquing my performance. As my anxiety with public speaking had not yet been overcome, this was a bit like throwing gasoline on my deepest fears! Furthermore, during the filming I had to adhere to a rigid set of rules and presentation techniques which were counter to my own inherent style. As I stood up to speak, my knees shook and my hands began to sweat. I did not feel authentic in the slightest—the whole thing felt unnatural in every way. I left the sales training meeting a wreck, wondering if it was too late to go back to school and study counseling, accounting, or *anything* but sales.

Over the next three years, I was determined to overcome the fear of speaking in public. After studying my peers, leaders, and other professional communicators, it became clear that the trick was to simply be authentic. I spoke from the heart, was transparent in who I was, and made no attempt to be something I was not. I started looking at public speaking opportunities as a moment to connect, not impress.

Just like my peers in that public speaking exercise who sacrificed themselves in favor of a slick presentation, companies, too, can look great on paper or from the podium, but very few organizations are what they seem when you look under the hood.

This is why corporate identity is so important; it is the driving force that separates you from the crowd. We have worked with a number of smaller and emerging companies in the world of packaged goods who operate from a different vantage point than their competitors: *Their corporate identity is fixed, and their business is an expression of their identity.* Their identity is clearer than their competitors' identities. In other words, corporate values really *do* matter, and they provide business differentiation.

A sculptor chips away at stone to uncover the creation within; likewise, one's identity is often buried inside, waiting to be discovered. We all have a unique identity, but it is often left buried within the stone of fear. Great leaders and organizations take a risk by listening to the voice within—stepping purposefully into their calling. The identity they find at their core is something they protect vigilantly.

However, many companies make this claim about corporate values, but it fails to manifest, as indicated by objective performance assessments with their employees and customers. I find in my consulting work that most companies haven't created a distinct identity, and the majority of them are struggling with team alignment. And this is always evident to the customer!

When identity is *fixed*, it is easy to attract leaders who have the capacity to carry the company's cause. The company doesn't rely on motivational incentives or management controls; instead, there is buy-in that is organic and authentic. This type of work culture breeds collaboration, creative tension, and purpose, and it allows the company to go places that competitors only wish they could.

What is your company's reason for being?

The best dark horse companies unleash ideas and express their identity through their business and their employees. The following are five examples of special organizations where *wha*t they do is at the root of *who* they are.

WIFFLE® BALL*
MORE THAN A PLASTIC BALL AND BAT

*WIFFLE, WIFFLE Ball, and the Yellow bat are registered trademarks of The Wiffle Ball, Inc.

I remember playing Wiffle ball for hours as a kid. The field had rocks and pot holes; there would be leaves burning and smoke blowing onto the field from the next-door neighbor's yard—but all that only added to the atmosphere for late evening baseball heroics. Even friends rotating in and out of the game never compromised the theatre of baseball. No matter the conditions, we made it work. But there was one exception: We had to have a Wiffle ball and yellow bat, or the game was off!

That skinny yellow bat had the power to catapult the whistling ball seemingly hundreds of feet over a makeshift fence. It could end a game late in the ninth inning after a four-run comeback at dusk. That bat and ball were irreplaceable; they had an *identity*.

In a digital world where the average grade school child invests eight to ten hours per week playing video games, or is overly invested in competitive traveling sports, shouldn't Wiffle ball have died out years ago? There is something about this product that pulls you back in, no matter what other sophisticated technologies are introduced. It's infectious, and it's an important part of our summer culture.

If you believe Wiffle ball is still a relevant brand that creates emotion, you would never suspect it is still made in the U.S., right? Yet, for over sixty years The Wiffle Ball Inc. in Connecticut—now led by brothers David and Stephen Mullany—has been manufacturing this still wildly popular brand. "We're very happy producing our products here. No reason we can't make a top-quality product here at an affordable price and stay in business," says David Mullany.[3]

In a world where the majority of low-cost manufacturing moved offshore decades ago, how can a little fifteen-person company still make Wiffle balls for the world? And more importantly, *why* do they do it? Because it's personal: fattening the bottom line at Wiffle Ball Inc. is far from the sole objective.

The company inspiration came from Stephen's grandfather's desire to design a lightweight ball that wouldn't destroy the neighbor's house—a caring, human-based product concept if there ever was one! The company is still family-run even though there have been many opportunities to sell Wiffle Ball Inc. to outsiders.

The Mullany family is grounded in the fundamentals of their business, and they truly enjoy working with each other. President David J. Mullany believes the essence of his business focuses on making a fairly priced honest product while supporting their retail partners that distribute his brand.[4]

Success at this company has less to do with personal finance than it does with identity, family, and fun.

WAHL HOME PRODUCTS
CONTINUOUS/OBSESSIVE IMPROVEMENT

Sterling, Illinois is a small town of less than 16,000 people in the western part of the state. The terrain is flat, surrounded by farmland,

The simplicity and passion of Wiffle Ball is buried in emotion and identity.
How can something so simple create such memories?

and is a stereotypical Midwest town. Sterling is also the home of Wahl Home Products, the leader in remarkably designed hair trimming and clipping products for professionals and consumers.

At the core of Wahl Home Products is a sense of responsibility to the Wahl family and its extended family of employees. CEO Greg Wahl says they have a responsibility to the hundreds of employees and families that make up this unique 100-year-old company. Trained as an engineer at Notre Dame, Wahl loves lean manufacturing principles, performance gaps, business constraints, problem solving, and process improvement. He is a self-described obsessive and "chief worrier" of the company, and

Cutting hair goes deep with the Wahl family and with President Greg Wahl (left), speaking with Bruce Kramer, VP of Sales and Marketing. The Wahl team is obsessed with product quality and culture.

he makes no bones about his quirky nature. In Greg's words, "No one has ever accused me of being normal."

Wahl says his leadership style was shaped, in part, by a deeply caring mother and a driven father who was often short on compliments. Greg emerged as a deeply caring leader who lives in fear of one day becoming obsolete. This combination of traits fuels the engine of innovation at the company.

I asked Greg to share his personal business mantra. He paused for a moment, and then stated, "I am obsessed with doing what's right for my company and family."[5]

Case in point: In late 2011, Wahl conducted an assessment of the company's work culture and discovered that 98.3 percent of all employees said Wahl Clipper Corporation is a wonderful place to work. Of 800-plus U.S.-based employees, only twelve people were not satisfied— which meant that Greg Wahl was not satisfied. "Those twelve people keep me up at night," he told me.

He joined the family business in 1977, was appointed COO in 1991, and president in 1997. Since 1996, the Wahl organization has grown

3.5 times in size. When he took over, the company was suffering from iron-clad silos which included lack of teamwork and poor communication between sales, marketing, and operations. Greg's philosophy of continuous improvement, problem solving, and tenacity has helped transform them into a company governed by rapid improvement sessions and meetings which he calls "collaborative consortiums." With typical humility, however, he admits there is work left to do. "Business and organizations are continuous learning and sharing of that learning. The reality is that I personally am very much a work in process relative to the future."

Despite being an engineer, Greg believes that success is never directly reflected in the numbers. While he may not be a man high on stage presence, Greg is a high-touch, high-love guy who cares deeply about his company and the families that make up his organization. There is great emotion in Greg's eyes as he shares the stories of his team's personal challenges and how he and his company have stepped in to provide relief to members of the company. Once Greg Wahl is involved with something, he is all in.

TRADITIONAL MEDICINALS:
BIGGER DOESN'T HAVE TO MEAN SELLING OUT

Teas have been consumed for more than 3,000 years, but a company in northern California is reintroducing Americans to the therapeutic benefits of the drink. For three decades, Traditional Medicinals has been creating teas with the purpose of providing affordable herbal medicine for family health and welfare.

Their corporate values include sustainability, ingredient purity, and social and environmental activism. Darrick Blinoff, Traditional Medicinals' sales leader, peppers his conversation with terms like "interdependence," "stewardship of the resources," and "systemic wellness." He firmly believes that business is a vehicle to educate and change the health and wellness model.

Blair Kellison, CEO of Traditional Medicinals, brings a financial and Nestle-branding background to this zealous corporation. He says they compete with the national brands—such as Celestial Teas and

Lipton—sitting on the shelf next to them by instilling "the values and mission of our small company into our team." For example, one of the company's values is a feeling of "obligation to inspire other companies on free-trade practices and to help the world with herbal self-care."

Traditional Medicinals has experienced double-digit growth for years and has battled competitors many times their size. Kellison says, "Everyone thinks that since you are growing you must be selling out. We think just the opposite. That is, once you get bigger you must be

Traditional Medicinals believe in influencing the course of other emerging companies through doing the right thing, such as free trade.

even tighter and even more disciplined with your mission and values. You have the stage, so now influence those around you."

Traditional Medicinals is an employee-owned company; they find that giving shares to their workers supports their commitment to the corporate vision. The company is rarely governed or directed by quarterly or even annual sales targets. That doesn't mean they don't have targets; they do, and they monitor them strictly. But their values, product quality, and passion for their customers are not put at risk by the demands of a quarterly sales number.

"We listen to both the company shareholders and stakeholders as a means of staying aligned within our culture," says Kellison. "We also stay emotionally connected to the brand—while also training our organization to stay relevant in the industry and with our retail customers. We really do believe in this corporate story, and my vision is that we can influence the course of other emerging companies." [6]

METHOD HOME INC.
A "PURPOSEFULLY WEIRD" CULTURE

In 2002, a Northern California company named Method Home Inc. was founded on the vision that business could be an agent of positive change as a source of solutions to social and environmental problems. Co-founders Eric Ryan and Adam Lowry created a brand and work culture founded on a compelling social mission.

Ryan, the company's brand architect, says, "Our mission is fundamentally different than most organizations, and our culture is purposefully weird. Our mission is to rid the world of dirty—whether it is dirty business practices, dirty materials, and even a dirty planet. We are trying to create an authentic mission and culture that disrupts the soap and cleaning category and makes a difference for the world."

Eric Ryan and Adam Lowry, co-founders of Method, with some of their distinctive soap dispensers they call "little agents of environmental change."

Ryan says his personal connection with the environment started with his love of sailing Lake Michigan, where he and Lowry, a chemical engineer and lead formula designer at Method, grew up. "We recently have been very inspired and even disturbed by the book *Plastic Ocean* authored by Charles Moore—there are five million pieces of plastic entering the ocean from the land each day!" The product development team at Method is recycling the plastic sea waste; within the company, they also call this process Save the Sushi or We Believe in Reincarnation. "This type of business really matters and inspires me," says Ryan.

The mission statement of Method Home Inc. reads: "Our challenge is to make sure that every product we send out into the world truly is a little agent of environmental change. Little green soldiers in the battle of doing-well-by-doing-good, if you will. We love to solve the technical riddles of making great cleaning products using green chemistry, user-centered design, and smart engineering, with our ultimate goal of brilliantly functional products that delight users and embody comprehensive sustainability." [7]

In late 2012, Method was acquired by European rival Ecover, allowing for a bigger European footprint and growth potential. Method has taken soap and turned it into a societal cause.

WHOLE FOODS
LIVE, BREATHE, EAT YOUR CORPORATE IDENTITY

There are only a handful of companies that actually have the influence to create a societal movement—not just reflecting the culture, but moving it in a different direction. One such cultural catalyst is Whole Foods, based in Austin, Texas.

Founded in 1980, this 300-store chain is the leader in natural and organic food. But more than that, Whole Foods is a leader in experiential food retailing for a zealous and emerging group of consumers. They live, breathe, and eat their corporate identity, purpose, and mission: Whole Foods—Whole People—Whole Planet.

How does Whole Foods achieve a culture of differentiation and high standards? It goes without saying that they procure great organic, sustainable, and healthy foods. But they do this through what they refer to as "whole people"—employees who are passionate about healthy food and a healthy planet. Members of each individual store team have the authority to bring on local products that meet the unique tastes of their community. Their decentralized team culture creates a highly motivated and high-performing organization.

Information is shared openly with all full-time team members, and it is obvious that team members have a deep understanding of the majority of products sitting on their shelves. Learning about new organic food products is not a mandatory task for members of their organization; it is part of their personal identity.

Whole Foods is deeply committed to helping take care of the planet, and they actively support organic farming and sustainable agriculture. The company assists global neighbors through their Whole Planet Foundation's micro-lending operations. Each individual store is involved in local causes through supporting food banks, sponsoring neighborhood events, and donating to local non-profit groups. [8]

In my own experience, I have seen close-up that when profit it the only score card, a culture of creativity cannot be sustained; from top to bottom, Whole Foods not only shares but lives by this sentiment. In his book *Conscious Capitalism*, John Mackey, the company's founder and Co-CEO, asserts that a healthy business is a catalyst for value creation and can positively transform culture. For years Mackey has argued that profit is never enough; profit doesn't inspire people, nor does it connect on the deepest level.

In order to fight the perception of profit as a company's primary objective and reclaim "capitalism" and "business" as positive words, businesses have to find a purpose beyond just making money. Profit is necessary for business, Mackey said, but it's necessary in the same way that the body needs to produce red blood cells: it's needed, but it's not the sole purpose.

It is also essential for the company to be conscious about creating value for every one of its stakeholders, to work for the benefit of employees, customers, investors, and suppliers, all at the same time to create a virtuous cycle.[9]

Many of us may be skeptical when we read mission and value statements posted in boardrooms and office lunchrooms. We have all been disappointed by words that do not match actions. I myself have seen leaders and organizations simply pay lip service to ideals they clearly don't adhere to; this charade does more to discourage company morale than anything else. These leaders would do well to realize that you don't need a printed vision statement on the wall if people can see your vision happening in your life and in your company.

As I discussed in this chapter, organizations such as Wiffle Ball Inc., Wahl Home Products, Method, Traditional Medicinals, and Whole Foods see business as personal, and it really does serve a larger purpose. And that purpose is understood by *everyone* involved with the company.

INSIGHTS ON IDENTITY

» "YOU DO NOT MERELY WANT TO BE CONSIDERED JUST THE BEST OF THE BEST. YOU WANT TO BE CONSIDERED THE ONLY ONES WHO DO WHAT YOU DO."

» DARK HORSE TEAMS OUTPERFORM THEIR LARGER COMPETITORS BECAUSE THEIR SENSE OF IDENTITY AND PURPOSE IS GREATER THAN THEIR DESIRE FOR RICHES.

» *"WHO DO WE INTEND TO BE?"* HOW YOU ANSWER THAT QUESTION PROVIDES A VALUABLE INSIGHT INTO AN ORGANIZATION'S LIKELIHOOD OF SUCCEEDING.

» THE BEST ORGANIZATIONS DON'T PRACTICE LEADERSHIP CONTROL; THEY TEACH OTHERS ABOUT CORE VALUES WHILE LIVING THEM.

» THE ESSENCE OF THE TOP EMERGING COMPANIES IS THAT THEIR IDENTITY IS FIXED; BUSINESS IS AN EXPRESSION OF THIS IDENTITY. THEIR BUSINESS IS VERY PERSONAL AND PURPOSEFUL, AND IT RUNS DEEP.

» WHEN IDENTITY IS FIXED, IT IS EASY TO ATTRACT LEADERS WHO HAVE THE CAPACITY TO CARRY THE COMPANY'S CAUSE. THERE IS BUY-IN THAT IS ORGANIC AND AUTHENTIC.

» MISSION STATEMENTS HANGING ON OFFICE WALLS ARE NOW OFFICIALLY DEAD; THE MISSION MUST BE SEEN IN THE DAY-TO-DAY ACTIONS OF AN ORGANIZATION.

THOUGHT STARTERS

1. DOES YOUR ORGANIZATION'S MISSION INSPIRE YOU, AND DOES IT SUPPORT YOUR PERSONAL IDENTITY?

2. IS THERE A CORPORATE CAUSE (OTHER THAN PROFIT) THAT UNDERPINS THE IDENTITY OF YOUR COMPANY?

3. WHAT TYPE OF NEW EMPLOYEES OR PRACTICES WOULD WIDEN THE GAP BETWEEN YOU AND YOUR COMPETITORS?

4. WOULD YOUR COMPETITORS BE ABLE TO CLEARLY DESCRIBE YOUR CORPORATE IDENTITY?

5. DO YOU HAVE AN IDENTITY OR POSITION THAT CLEARLY DIFFERENTIATES YOU FROM YOUR COMPETITION?

6. WOULD EVERYONE IN YOUR ORGANIZATION BE ABLE TO CLEARLY COMMUNICATE THE VISION AND PURPOSE OF YOUR TEAM?

7. CAN YOU LOOK IN THE MIRROR AND SAY THAT YOU ARE THE ONLY ONES WHO DO WHAT YOU DO?

8. WHAT ARE THE THREE LARGEST STRATEGIC ROADBLOCKS OR BLIND SPOTS LIMITING YOUR GROWTH?

Chapter 2:

ALIGNMENT

Outward Focus on the Customer

Half the world is composed of people who have something to say and can't, and the other half who have nothing to say and keep on saying it.

—**ROBERT FROST, POET**

Do your customers fall into the camp of "having something to say, but can't," because you aren't listening? We live in a corporate culture where today's success does not guarantee future success; there are no longer periods of calm seas for leaders in any industry. In fact, the more established your organization, the more at risk you may be to a dark horse sneaking up on you.

The key to becoming and staying an industry leader lies in the alignment of your organization's strategy, people, and systems while understanding your customers *unstated* needs. Recently I was speaking with a chief executive about helping him uncover business blind spots between him and his top customers. He shared with me that he fully believes his customers are telling him the unfiltered truth about his company's performance. He went on to share with me that his relationships are strong and that his customers share what's on their mind. This top executive believed he had it all under control.

I loved his aspirational thinking, but dark horses tend to evaluate things in a more honest fashion—the facts in this fellow's case showed something very different. We all have blind spots, and most people, especially if they are not in an intimate relationship, withhold negative feedback out of fear of conflict or hurting one's feelings. The truth is that most of the time, we do not get the full truth on our personal performance, because others are not comfortable sharing the truth.

Booz & Company consultants recently surveyed more than 1,800 executives from different sized companies and different industries about their companies' strategies, decision making, priorities, and growth potential. Only 13 percent of respondents felt their company could be deemed "coherent" (that is, in alignment).

Digging into the data a little deeper, the cracks in the armor really start to show:

» 53 PERCENT OF EMPLOYEES DO NOT FEEL THEIR COMPANY'S STRATEGY WILL LEAD TO SUCCESS.

» 67 PERCENT SAY THEIR COMPANY'S CAPABILITIES DO NOT FULLY SUPPORT THE COMPANY'S STRATEGY, NOR DOES THEIR STRATEGY CREATE VALUE.

» ONLY 21 PERCENT THINK THEIR COMPANY HAS A RIGHT TO WIN IN ALL THE MARKETS IT COMPETES IN. IN OTHER WORDS, THE COMPANY IS EXPANDING INTO NEW BUSINESSES THEY ARE NOT RESOURCED OR CAPABLE OF SUCCEEDING WITH, OR DON'T HAVE THE CAPABILITIES TO TRULY OFFER A UNIQUE SOLUTION TO THE CUSTOMER.[1]

This level of internal lack of alignment obviously limits growth, but it also hinders top employee retention, motivation, and loyalty to the cause.

Internal motivation and commitment is a byproduct of believing in something; this requires authenticity. When you doubt what you believe in, you lose influence and effectiveness. Alignment is important to success, and it is even more important in a world of hyper-competition. We must also remember that alignment is not simply a technique, but a genuine outward focus. For me, it involves showing up to work each day, ready to deliver whatever my employees might need.

Are you as aligned as you think you are?

When I started Elevation Forum (more on that in Chapter 8), I wanted to create an atmosphere for those in command to discuss their struggles in order to become better leaders. But the forum is all about helping companies, not simply leaders, grow. For dark horse companies, passion, thought leadership, and corporate identity really matter to the retailers that carry their products, the consumers who purchase them, and the employees who work at these companies. These organizations instinctively understand how to connect and engage all of these constituents on both an emotional level and a functional level.

An effort must be made to stay on top of what really matters. From my own experience, I could name a number of things that are not in alignment, which is why I personally utilize a coach to keep me in alignment in my personal and business life.

Far from turning a blind eye, dark horse leaders accumulate and incorporate unstated or whispered customer insights into the fabric of their business. These leaders are often not in the mainstream; they are frequently characterized as being "before their time." I recently sat down and interviewed several of the top merchandising executives at leading retailers in America. One senior buyer told me that "Way too many sales and marketing executives are flying blind" to the needs of buyers.

ROADBLOCKS TO ALIGNMENT

The following are four alignment roadblocks uncovered during my research and the longer-term implications of not addressing each roadblock.

Roadblock #1: You Don't Understand My Agenda: Many executives don't really understand their customers' most valuable priorities—their personal and professional agendas—and focus too much of their time prescribing solutions instead of understanding their customers' areas of corporate dissatisfaction. Valuable business opportunities get left on the table as a result.

Most of us are loyal to a few service companies which have taken the time to create an emotional connection with us. But more than that, we are loyal to companies that *listen* intently to our deepest needs and uncover opportunities we may not be consciously aware of. In other words, these companies have a true outward focus; that focus is on us, the consumer. They understand that customers want to eliminate problems, not buy products.

Roadblock #2: You Don't Provide Real Differentiation from the Competition: Most executives I've interviewed believe that sales and marketing leaders are not fully prepared to do business on the customer's terms, and are not providing enough meaningful value and differentiation. They are guilty of overvaluing their proposition and underestimating their competitors while running blind to their company's weaknesses. Now that is a dangerous combination!

My survey revealed that most companies and brands are much more replaceable and vulnerable than they think. In a world of micro-differentiation and value brands, the average consumer does not see the difference in most products and will easily move to a competing brand.

We now live in a world where the average drugstore has more than 22,000 items on the shelf, and the average food store has 45,000 items,

We now live in a world of too many choices; retailers chase after each other trying to stay competitive, and manufacturers are playing following the leader.

but the average home has less than 400 unique items in its cupboards. That's a huge gap between demand and need, and most people will never buy or consume the majority of items available in the market.

We now live in a world of too many choices; retailers chase after each other trying to stay competitive, and manufacturers are playing following the leader.

Roadblock #3: Not Utilizing All Assets: Things are changing so quickly in the market today that consumers are realizing they don't know what they don't know. This amounts to a great opportunity for people who educate, facilitate, and co-create new business ventures. Executives must learn to create value outside of their product offering and utilize *all* their tangible and intangible assets in order to differentiate the customers.

Roadblock #4: Not Listening: We also found that 80 percent of executive buyers interviewed stated that many leading sales and marketing leaders don't listen or effectively read between the lines during their engagements. Companies that remain in alignment listen not only to what is said, but subtleties left unsaid—"whispered insights." A great business cannot be afraid of the truths these insights afford. As one leading executive shared with me, "Too often sales and marketing executives leave the impression of working off of a script." The fact is that an attentive ear is far more useful than a big mouth.

In my time as a consultant, it seems the most aligned firms I've encountered spend an enormous amount of time pausing, thinking, and analyzing their business. Dark horse companies that out-strategize their larger competitors are adept at uncovering and fixing their customers' problems, known or otherwise. They go deeper—always questioning, never assuming. How do they achieve a position of superior knowledge and customer clarity?

» THEY INVEST THEIR DEEPEST THINKERS AND BEST ACHIEVERS ON THEIR MOST VALU-
   ABLE CUSTOMER ACCOUNTS.
» THEY INSTALL A DISCIPLINED SALES DISCOVERY PROCESS THAT UNCOVERS
   CUSTOMER GAPS.
» THEY ALLOW TIME FOR PERSONAL AND CORPORATE REFLECTION, AND ENCOURAGE
   ALL MEMBERS OF THE TEAM TO PROVIDE INSIGHT TO THE CUSTOMER.
» THEY MAY USE EITHER FORMAL OR INFORMAL "WAR ROOMS" TO CONDUCT WEEKLY
   STRATEGY MEETINGS WITH CORE MEMBERS OF THEIR TEAMS.
» THEY ARE COMFORTABLE BLENDING STRATEGIC THINKING AND HARD-HITTING
   EXECUTION DISCUSSIONS WITHIN THE SAME MEETING.

Staying in deep alignment with your top customers takes heart, astute listening skills, and proficiency in assessing the changing landscape of our business. I will share five unique organizations that have mastered this art form.

APOLLO HEALTH AND BEAUTY CARE INC.
CUSTOMER ALIGNMENT AS ART FORM

Apollo Health and Beauty Care Inc., one of the premier manufacturers of private brand health and personal care products, is a privately held company that creates unique brands for individual retailers. It is difficult enough to create a brand and market it on a national level; to design customized brands that align with a retailer's vision, consumers' tastes, and do it all on a limited-run basis—that is an art form!

Apollo was founded and is led by executive twin brothers Charles and Richard Wachsberg. Since 1993, their company has distributed and marketed customized exclusive brand designs for many of the top retailers in the U.S., Canada, and Central and South America. Apollo is known as an elegant company that takes pride in creating formulations that are often better than and ahead of the trend in the broad health and beauty sector. Safeway stores has partnered numerous times with Apollo on custom portfolios of products under numerous brand names including the In-Kind name, available at retail outlets for a number of years.

In-Kind hand soap, body wash, shampoos, and conditioners are an example of Apollo's classy approach in designing retailer specific innovation. Looks like a national brand, doesn't it?

Charles shared with me that Apollo doesn't just work with their customers; they build deeply aligned, long-term partnerships with their retail clients. "We don't simply make products for our retail partners," he says. "We focus on selling services, creating purposeful alignment, while helping our cherished clients build *their* brands. We don't believe that our retail clients need us to be myopic, task-oriented suppliers; they need partners with longer term vision and they need to understand who owns and runs the company. That makes it personal." Charles says he relishes the privilege to be the face of Apollo Health and Beauty Care for their customers. He continued: "We hire people who love to please their customers. Every day we are entrusted with our client's vision, and our job is to understand that vision and create both inspirational and aspirational solutions that are relevant for their consumers.

"We don't pick our customers; they select us—and with that decision comes a great responsibility to create something elegant and worthy. You can only achieve this by thinking big, while managing execution and details on the ground level."

While Charles and his brother Richard do the investing and take on the risk, decisions are balanced by clients and the 500 associates within the Apollo family. Recently, Apollo opened their new state-of-the-art facility in Toronto, and the design of the corporate campus was implemented with the voice of the client and the associates in mind. The manufacturing and corporate offices were strategically relocated ten minutes from the old facility, next to the railroads which will unload bulk ingredients for the many product formulas mixed and produced in the facility. "When we built our new facility," says Charles, "we shared almost every decision with our employees to ensure alignment throughout the process. We asked our team to provide advice as to space functionality and form prior to designing and finalizing plans.

The Apollo worldwide manufacturing and design facility supports the identity of Apollo: elegant, precise, and deeply personalized. The company mirrors the custom solutions they design for their retail clients.

We needed and valued this consensus as it was important to have our team help create this workplace experience. We have a transparent culture that promotes dialogue and which challenges prevailing wisdom in favor of smarter, more contemporary solutions. We treat this business as a democracy. The best and most relevant idea always wins." [2]

DO THEY ACTUALLY WANT/NEED WHAT YOU'RE SELLING?

Another effective practice is to constantly ask your customers whether or not what you offer actually matters to them. Makes sense, right? But many organizations sell what's in their cupboard, rather than figuring out what products they should stock in their cupboards in the first place.

The best doctors and medical facilities spend an appropriate amount of time consulting with specialists and using technology to diagnose a patient before prescribing medical solutions. Winning companies can operate in a similar fashion with their customers; for example, by conducting comprehensive discovery meetings with their top customers prior to creating a new product or service. This diagnostic process allows both parties to co-create the next generation of products, with the best interests of everyone at heart.

The most successful companies are unafraid of asking difficult questions of their customers. In fact, they thrive on hearing bad news because it provides them with an opportunity to step up and fix a problem. Business leaders themselves must be unafraid to ask penetrating questions that facilitate a deeper understanding of the customer's needs; only then can a diagnosis be made.

NOW FOODS
LISTENING IN THE FICKLE WORLD OF NATURAL HEALTH

One company that's adept at diagnosing customer opportunities and then designing solutions is NOW Foods in Bloomingdale, Illinois. The leader in natural vitamins and supplements, NOW Foods tries to keep their ears open to consumer whispers in the ever-changing, fickle world of natural health products.

NOW Foods lives in a constant state of assessing the emerging needs of the natural consumer, and makes vitamins, natural personal care products, and sports nutrition products.

How does a smaller company like NOW Foods play in a sector dominated by billion-dollar health care companies? The answer is that they have a deep understanding of their consumers' needs; they listen with passion, and are rarely surprised by what's coming in their market.

Started in 1968 as a small soy products manufacturer, NOW Foods was founded on the belief that good health should not be a luxury available only to the wealthy. They've made it their life's work to offer health foods and nutritional supplements of the highest quality at prices that are fair and affordable. Today, NOW Foods is one of the top-selling brands in health foods stores, and they are an award-winning manufacturer—one of the largest natural products manufacturers in the U.S. They are also a respected advocate of the natural product industry and a leader in the fields of nutritional science and methods development.

This company is in a constant state of listening to their customers, employees, partners, retailers, and vendors; they are always on the lookout for emerging ideas, new product trends, and consumer shifts in the consumption of vitamins, minerals, and other natural health supplements. They are in a state of never arriving, of learning, adapting, and rarely losing opportunities.

Dan Richard, NOW Foods' national sales manager and son of founder Elwood Richard, shared with me an example of how their boutique retail stores provide a special type of customer intimacy.

"We operate eleven Fruitful Yield health stores in the Chicago area; each store is packed with NOW Foods brands, but also markets many of the top health food products and vitamins offered in much larger outlets such as Whole Foods. These customized outlets conduct health screenings for their patrons, offer fresh organic foods, and serve as a product laboratory for NOW Foods. As you walk into these stores, each

Fruitful Yield uses their smaller, intimate natural foods stores to understand the emerging needs and desires of their health and wellness consumer.

employee is impeccably trained on emerging health care items and understands the unique specifications of each item on the shelf."[3]

NOW Foods doesn't move a muscle unless their most valued retail partners and consumers tell them to move. Their corporate culture and leadership values are to listen more than speak, and their attention to other's voices creates competitive advantage and alignment throughout their industry. NOW Foods celebrates and listens to the voice of everyone.

INCORPORATE INFLUENCERS

The most valuable dark horse companies get everyone, including senior management, third-party relationships, and any other people of influence to engage and create value with their top customers. Involving your senior-level leaders in the sales development process with no set strategy or plan of action can introduce a number of problems including unclear meeting roles, too many theatrics, or poor meeting structure. However, when senior corporate influencers are utilized properly—with clearly defined roles and tasks—it enables growth and deeper customer alignment.

Here is a principle understood by winning dark horse companies: *Everyone is in sales and everyone does marketing.* In other words, whether you work in manufacturing, design, finance, logistics, or customer service, you are responsible for supporting and developing a long-standing, profitable customer relationship.

In the most aggressive, relevant organizations, everybody is listening, selling, thinking, and looking for ideas to build stronger relationships and solutions for the customer. And that's why I love this next company.

REVIVE PERSONAL BRANDS
IT'S ABOUT CREATING SOMETHING BEAUTIFUL

Revive Personal Brands in Madison, New Jersey, creates innovative oral care and sexual health items, including Stim-U-Dent plaque removers, Fresh 'n Brite dual-layer denture cleaner, the Natural Dentist, and the Options sexual health product line. All items are unique in positioning under huge competitive pressures—and succeeding.

Revive's President and Chief Operating Officer is the fiery and energizing Kelly Kaplan. She helped build and sell another underdog company Dental Concepts, and has supported the marketing efforts of a number of top brands in her career including The Doctor's NightGuard, Kaopectate, Nuprin, Centrum, Slim Fast, and Dexatrim. Kaplan acquired Revive Personal Brands in 2008 and has almost doubled its size since. I asked her how she accomplished this feat; in her typical style, she responded:

"Business is about people and it is about passion and love; it is about creating something beautiful. I love what I am doing and really want to create a great team who enjoys being with each other while creating products that help others make great choices."

Kaplan's mentor and partner is Revive's CEO, Mike Lesser, who operates from the same center as Kaplan. He has built, run, and

Revive Personal Brands is all about intimacy—and not just in the function of their oral care and sexual health products. They are intimate in their customer relationships.

sold several companies, but after a short-lived retirement (the only thing he's ever failed at, notes Kaplan), he joined with his protégé to form Revive Personal Brands.

Revive goes deeper in terms of passion for and commitment to customers than any dark horse company I have seen. Kaplan believes that organizations win not only with skills, but with love.[4] She is

Kelly Kaplan, President, and Mike Lesser, CEO of Revive Personal Brands, preach culture, intimacy, authenticity, and playing for the future. Revive is a dark horse company that wins based on the little things.

relentless in her new item preparation prior to discussing ideas with a customer. I have seen her, after a twelve-hour sales conference, hand-write forty cards to her customers while most people are in bed or out having a drink. She wanted to ensure that the note—personal, specific, passionate, and authentic—was on the customer's desk within forty-eight hours.

Does Kaplan believe in market research? Absolutely. Does she rely solely on these insights? Never. She assertively listens to the consumer and puts herself into situations to get to the truth of her company, her associates, and her brands.

She does not take negative criticism personally—a major reason why her customers are advocates of her business and brands. They are emotionally connected to Kaplan personally, and go out of their way to coach and collaborate with her on her next set of new items. One colleague of Kaplan told me, "I have seen her intense love of her brands and company *win deals that she didn't deserve to win*, based on the apparent integrity and passion she brought to the engagement. People want her to be successful, because she is that good of a person."

GET TO THE ROOT CAUSE

Most organizations have blind spots hindering their growth and alignment with their top customers and partners. So what is the root of this recurring leadership trap? In many cases, executives are fearful of true self-assessment that would reveal cracks in their own armor, while others might not place a high enough value on personal reflection and honest criticism.

How often do most organizations honestly look in the mirror? A recent Gallup poll shows that only 29 percent of the workforce is actually engaged and committed to the cause in the workplace. This means two-thirds of the workforce really is not in the game. Yikes! This is a blind spot for some executives and a frustration for many of the rest. Uncommitted, uninspired employees don't go unnoticed by customers.

Years ago, I worked with an executive--I'll spare him the embarrassment of calling him out by name--who administered a feedback process with members of his team, but would not subject himself to the same level of discipline. At one point he made himself vulnerable to critique, didn't like the outcome, and never asked for it again. He was not strong enough to deal with the truth. He was not an effective leader.

Unfortunately, this seems to be a recurring theme I've encountered in my work as a consultant. Alignment has got to be from the top down; no one in the company ought to be exempt. If I'm unable to so much as reach the company's president—no matter how enthusiastic everyone else might be—then all is for naught.

DEFINE THE PROBLEM FIRST

The tendency of most people is to provide a solution before understanding the opportunity. Einstein was once asked: if you had one hour to save the world, how would you spend the time? He responded,

"I would spend the first fifty-five minutes defining the problem, and the last five minutes finding the solution."

CAN YOU BRING CLARITY TO THE CUSTOMER?

Winning dark horse companies do not show up in front of their customers with multiple, divergent strategies; they present a clear corporate brand image, a focused strategy, and a crisp solution. The overriding goal is to create a competitive position where you are the *only ones who do what you do.* The more clarity an organization brings to their customer engagements, the higher the probability of winning.

Soothing, Naturally Effective Relief

Ricola AG has created a special brand identity while emphasizing an outward focus on their consumers and retail partners.

RICOLA AG KEEPING THEIR HEADS IN THE MOUNTAINS

Switzerland's Ricola AG, which makes an array of herbal cough and throat drops exported to more than fifty countries, is a family-owned company centered on economically, socially, and ecologically sustainable management philosophies. Aside from a clear brand message, corporate alignment with a number of their top retail partners is key to Ricola's success.

The American operation of Ricola is led by industry veteran Bill Higgins, who emphasizes collaborative, higher-level engagement with all of his retail partners. Ricola leadership gets intimately involved with new item presentations, sharing emerging trends with the consumer while bringing forward new formulas, flavors, and new packages. "We stay aligned by listening intently to the needs and views of our top retail partners," says Higgins. "They help us understand what's coming around the corner, and we are only as good as these key partnerships. I am passionate about being involved with each of our top retail customers. I do my best not to overstep my boundaries, but I want them to know me, and feel our identity."

Ricola has a firm understanding of their identity: "We're a family business which is authentically a family," says Higgins. "Many larger companies acquire family businesses and integrate them into the fold, and three years later they have lost their identity and authenticity. We hold tightly to the Swiss heritage and the imagery of our brand, which is an alternative herbal remedy. Everyone in our corporate home is aligned with this identity and we really do believe it and value it."

Executive team meetings are often hosted in chalets in the mountains of Switzerland. These meetings occur several times each year, and this beautiful locale is both a reward and a vehicle to keep everyone grounded in the ethos of the business. "When you look out of the window and see the land where our farmers harvest their herbs, it is a clear reminder that Ricola is attempting to blend the health and wellness of Switzerland and the modern world," says Higgins.

He continues: "We have built a very collaborative relationship because you can't fire family. You have to figure out all alternatives and you have to learn when to give and compromise. We believe in the third alternative—your idea, my idea, and our idea." [5]

BEIERSDORF USA
PLAYING THE CHALLENGER ROLE

I recently sat down with Bill Graham, President and General Manager of Beiersdorf North America. He's classy, studious, and disciplined; seemingly low key in public, but passionate to the core. Beiersdorf comprises great brands, with their centerpieces being Nivea, Eucerin, and Aquaphor skin care products. "We aspire to be recognized by our customers and doctors as the leading and most trusted experts in skin care," says Graham. "We play a challenger role in the U.S. We compete head-to-head in a number of skin care categories with some of the largest, resource-laden beauty companies in the world, such as P&G, Johnson & Johnson, L'Oréal, and Unilever. Given our scale and limited resources, we can't play the game in the open field, so we must 'move and improve,' embracing ambiguity and moving faster than our larger competitors. This is how we stay deeply aligned with our customers.

"Our success in the role as challenger, both now and into the future, requires that we have a clear focus, while intently listening and collaborating with our top retail partners," he says. "We are a lean organization, getting the right people and ensuring folks are in the right roles is most critical. The people who thrive at Beiersdorf are those who challenge the status quo, are passionate about winning, accountable, relentless about learning, and comfortable in a more entrepreneurial environment."

Another differentiating attribute of Beiersdorf is the close collaboration they have across functions, particularly sales and marketing. "We are fortunate to have many smart employees that have a knack for finding new and unique ways to passionately compete in an incredibly competitive and dynamic market," says Graham. "Our team has an unmatched fighting spirit, and is not afraid of making mistakes, providing a terrific strategic advantage."

Graham reminded me, "There is not a playbook for winning consistently in today's market, but our company focus is emphasizing listening to the consumer, collaborating with the retail customer, and our 'move and improve' philosophy helps us stay on track."[6] Given Beiersdorf's recognition over the last several years as Supplier of the Year by many of North America's top retailers, this would certainly seem to be the case.

Beiersdorf USA plays a "challenger role" to the giant beauty companies who dwarf them in size and advertising investment.

WINNING UNDER PRESSURE

There is more pressure and hyper-competition than ever in the history of American business. So how do we optimize our business, develop our organizations, and provide value to our customers, all while maintaining alignment?

In his book *Better Under Pressure,* Justin Menkes writes that the top executives he has studied are best able to win during times of extreme pressure because they demonstrate these three core values:

1. **REALISTIC OPTIMISM.** "LEADERS WITH THIS TRAIT POSSESS CONFIDENCE WITH- OUT SELF-DELUSION OR IRRATIONALITY. THEY GO AFTER BIG IDEAS WHILE STAYING GROUNDED IN THE REALITY ALL AROUND THEM."
2. **SUBSERVIENCE TO PURPOSE.** "LEADERS WITH THIS ABILITY SEE THEIR PROFESSIONAL GOAL AS *SO PROFOUND* IN IMPORTANCE THAT THEIR LIVES BECOME MEASURED IN VALUE BY HOW MUCH THEY CONTRIBUTE TO FURTHERING THAT GOAL."
3. **FINDING ORDER IN CHAOS.** "LEADERS WITH THIS TRAIT FIND TAKING ON MULTIDIMENSIONAL PROBLEMS TO BE INVIGORATING, AND THEIR ABILITY TO BRING CLARITY TO QUANDARIES THAT BAFFLE OTHERS MAKES THEIR CONTRIBUTIONS INVALUABLE."[7]

These types of leaders create the atmosphere for people to unleash their unique assets and cultivate a culture of alignment. The ability to *fail* gracefully, often, and honestly, has never mattered more. Corporate cultures that thrive in chaos demonstrate resilience and are better suited to win in this new economy. That is their secret formula for staying in alignment.

INSIGHTS ON ALIGNMENT

»   YOU HAVE THE KEY TO GROWTH IF YOUR STRATEGY, PEOPLE, AND SYSTEMS ALIGN
    WITH YOUR CUSTOMERS.

»   MISALIGNMENT HINDERS EMPLOYEE RETENTION AND MOTIVATION. INTERNAL
    MOTIVATION AND COMMITMENT IS A BYPRODUCT OF BELIEVING IN
    SOMETHING. WHEN YOU DOUBT WHAT YOU BELIEVE IN, YOU LOSE INFLUENCE
    AND EFFECTIVENESS.

»   DARK HORSE LEADERS INCORPORATE WHISPERED CUSTOMER INSIGHTS INTO
    THEIR BUSINESS.

»   ROADBLOCKS TO ALIGNMENT ARE NOT UNDERSTANDING CUSTOMERS' AGENDAS,
    NOT DIFFERENTIATING FROM COMPETITORS, NOT OFFERING UNIQUE ASSETS THAT
    MATTER, AND NOT LISTENING.

»   GO DEEPER IN CUSTOMER ENGAGEMENTS, BLEND STRATEGY AND EXECUTION, AND
    INCLUDE SOCIETAL AND BUSINESS INFLUENCERS IN DISCUSSIONS.

»   DARK HORSE COMPANIES DIAGNOSE PROBLEMS (SIMILAR TO DOCTORS) BEFORE
    PRESCRIBING SOLUTIONS, AND THEN FIX THOSE PROBLEMS.

»   THE TOP EXECUTIVES (AND THE MOST ALIGNED) DEMONSTRATE REALISTIC OPTI-
    MISM, SUBSERVIENT TO PURPOSE, AND FIND ORDER IN CHAOTIC SITUATIONS.

THOUGHT STARTERS

1. HAVE YOU ASKED YOUR TOP CUSTOMERS ABOUT YOUR BLIND SPOTS?

2. DO YOU TRULY UNDERSTAND YOUR CUSTOMERS' MOST VALUABLE AGENDAS OR HIGHEST VALUE OBJECTIVES?

3. WHAT IS HINDERING YOUR GROWTH AND INTERNAL ALIGNMENT?

4. WHERE ARE YOU WASTING VALUABLE INTERNAL RESOURCES AND WHAT SHOULD YOU DO TO REDUCE THE EFFORT BEHIND THESE ACTIVITIES?

5. GIVEN YOUR CURRENT ASSETS, WHAT ADDITIONAL PRODUCTS CAN YOU MAKE WITH YOUR EXISTING TECHNOLOGIES?

6. ARE THERE UNIQUE UNMET NEEDS THAT YOUR COMPANY SHOULD EVALUATE AND SEIZE?

7. HOW DO YOU BELIEVE YOU ARE PERCEIVED BY YOUR CUSTOMERS? WOULD THEY STATE THAT YOU ARE ALIGNED WITH THEIR GOALS?

8. WHERE ARE YOU AT RISK, AND HOW DO YOU MINIMIZE COMPETITIVE THREATS?

You cannot depend on your eyes when your imagination is out of focus.

—MARK TWAIN

Chapter 3:

HIDDEN

ASSETS (WIN WITH IDEAS)

It was once stated in *The Economist* that 70 percent of the value of a new car lies in its intangibles.[1] The perceived impression or image of any item is often the primary driver of value. Pragmatists may struggle with this idea, but perception is all there is. It is a great reminder that companies and brands are made up of impressions, insights, and ideas.

We are operating in an economy where most things can be copied, replicated, and stolen before the commercialization process even begins. That is a frightening thought, especially for innovative companies that invest in research and development but are not adept at protecting their intellectual property. Innovation is vital to corporate health, as is stockpiling and protecting relevant intellectual properties that can be used with strategic customers.

There is no question that today we are in an idea era where every model, product, or solution is truly up for grabs. We are living in bipolar times: the largest companies are acquiring valuable pieces of smaller organizations to help differentiate their enterprise, and many upstart companies are creating innovation in their backyards, hoping to eventually be purchased or else, one day, to look like the shark that is trying to acquire them.

More often than not, winning organizations--no matter their size--*win with ideas.* They dig deep into the minds of their employees and pull out knowledge and insights; they offer precise solutions to problems faced by their customers.

Just how do idea-powered companies position themselves versus competitors?

» THEY SET THE RULES OF ENGAGEMENT IN THEIR INDUSTRY; THEY EARN THE ROLE OF OPINION LEADERS WITH THEIR CUSTOMERS AND THE INFLUENCERS THAT SUPPORT THEM.
» THEY TRANSFORM THE CUSTOMER RELATIONSHIP FROM TANGIBLE PRODUCTS TO A BLEND OF TANGIBLE AND INTANGIBLE, ADDED-VALUE, *KNOWLEDGE-BASED SERVICES.* THEY BRING IDEAS THAT TRANSFORM THEIR CUSTOMERS' BUSINESS.
» THEY *CO-CREATE SOLUTIONS* RIGHT ALONGSIDE THEIR RETAILER PARTNERS. (SEE CHAPTER 5.)

IDEAS ON SUNDAY MORNING

An offbeat example of thought leadership manifesting itself on both ends of the spectrum can be seen on any Sunday morning in many vibrant churches in America—in both the megachurches and the non-denominational upstart churches.

The megachurches with communities numbering upwards of 20,000 worshippers look more like small villages. But don't be misled by their size; many of these churches use transformational approaches to teach and minister to their flocks. Their campuses include integrated book-stores, restaurants, childcare, entertainment experiences, and break-through leadership conferences led by some of the strongest visionaries in our culture.

Two notable examples of megachurches are Saddleback Church in Southern California, led by Rick Warren, and Willow Creek in the northwest suburbs of Chicago, Illinois, led by head pastor Bill Hybels. Both men are transformational leaders who win with ideas, execute customer segmentation strategy, and create committed communities on a very high level. Their growing communities are healthy and make a difference in many people's lives. Knowledge is being communicated, values created, and lives changed. (Churches can be great case studies that, unfortunately, many companies miss).

On the other side of the religious spectrum is the growth of less traditional, small faith communities that meet in people's homes. These "house churches" are birthed out of individual needs unmet by traditional denominational values. Often these churches use a different strategy: *intimacy and a sense of community*. Many of these churches have cultivated such an experience that they become surrogate families to many people who feel alone in society.

Both styles of church are playing on very different assets, and both are thriving. They don't look like each other... *on purpose!* They are differentiated at such a high level that they must co-exist because each cannot, by their own inherent nature, compete with each other. I believe this church example shows how the rules of engagement are up for review and debate.

Similarly, dark horse companies can make this transition to become idea merchants as long as they have the requisite identity, alignment, passion, and willingness to embrace paradox and change.

SET THE RULES OF ENGAGEMENT

As most kids will tell you, he who gets to the park first gets to pick the teams and set the rules. Whether we realize it or not, this same principle is played out daily in all forms of business and life in general.

The principle is a variation of what is called *social proof*, a term coined by social scientist Robert Cialdini. His research shows that *we determine what is correct by finding out what other people think is correct*. We view a behavior in a given situation to the degree that we see others performing it.[2] In other words, once someone of influence sets the rules, it is very difficult to move the game to another park. Winning companies set the rules of engagement in such a way that they benefit their business model and their positioning in the market. That's a real home-field advantage!

IDEAS DIFFERENTIATE

Most of us feel comfortable buying things--a car, music, clothes, property, even services. If we can see it, feel it, and if it engages our senses, then we are generally okay with purchasing it. But intangibles are a whole different ballgame. We tend to underestimate or devalue intangible items, such as ideas, knowledge, and insights.

When I have to purchase legal advice, consulting direction, or even training and development, I fall into the same trap. I want to make it a transaction versus realizing that I am actually acquiring something as valuable, if not more valuable, than a tangible product.

Tangible things wear out; ideas can sustain and even transform a company. In many ways, great ideas or intangible assets can transform a life, an organization, and even a generation. Your company's ideas may be as valuable as your products.

The meanings poured into a brand name—the feelings generated when you associate with a group, cause, or idea—are examples of intangibles creating attachment or loyalty. The actual design of Tiger Woods' baseball cap is not that much better than alternatives; it's the Nike swoosh logo that creates the distinction. The logo is the brand, and it is an intangible that means something and attracts us. It stands for something, and that creates loyalty.

In the world of pop culture, few are more loyal and devoted than the die-hard fans of a rock band, and winning artists know how to brand

HIDDEN INTANGIBLE "ASSETS"

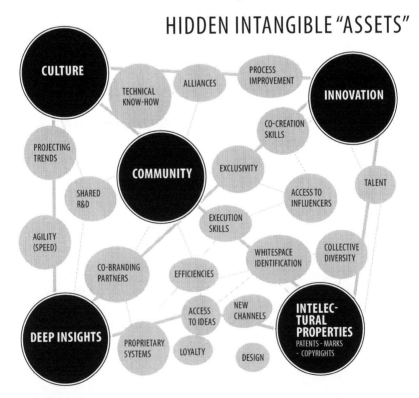

themselves with a clever balance of compelling art and sincerity. The band Switchfoot, for example, is known for crafting memorable guitar riffs and energetic live performances. What's more, they use their musical platform to champion the social causes they believe in--such as debt relief and homeless youth in their home town of San Diego--not for commercial gain, but because of a larger calling. This is just the sort of intangible quality that turns casual listeners into fanatics, members of something bigger than themselves.

Winning companies, too, are often differentiated by their intangible, or hidden, assets. These organizations value the things we, as consumers, value; they provide us with experiences and moments we don't forget. At this, there is no one better than Zappos.

ZAPPOS
SHOPPING MADE TOLERABLE FOR MEN

For most men, looking for a pair of shoes is a time consuming, tedious experience. Men would rather put this decision aside, delegate it to a loved one, or shelve it altogether. But then Zappos entered the market, and purchasing a pair of shoes suddenly became tolerable. Now owned by Amazon, Zappos is an online shoe and apparel shop known for creating memorable customer experiences, such as unmatched product variety, free shipping, effortless free returns up to one year, and a twenty-four-hour call center. This organization looks for ways to please!

The essence of the Zappos culture is the feeling of authentic commitment to the consumer. The corporate culture is committed to humility, passion, a little weirdness, open mindedness, family spirit, and those "wow" moments of service. Each of these attributes has nothing to do with products or bricks and mortar: these are intangible assets.

MORE WINNING WITH IDEAS

Whole Foods is a retailer with many tangible assets, but one of their most valuable assets is intangible: the zeal and brand knowledge of their employees. The typical Whole Foods employee understands the community mission of the store, and embodies the essence of its core values, including alignment with the larger societal green movement. And let's face it: passion to serve, educate, and create meaningful experiences is not exactly the first thing that comes to mind when you think about retailers.

On another level, the more distinct the hidden assets of a company, the deeper the commitment and personal connection the consumer has to their brands. We have found that there are four main areas where corporate assets hide:

1. KNOWLEDGE
2. PRODUCT/SERVICE CUSTOMIZATION
3. CONNECTORS
4. CUSTOMER EXPERIENCE

KNOWLEDGE

Knowledge is the most undervalued and underappreciated intangible asset within most organizations. We often think of intellectual properties as protectable assets locked up in the legal department--think patents, trademarks, copyrights. But knowledge goes much deeper and has broader tentacles. Organizations have large pools of knowledge locked up in business units, departments, and other members of the team.

Knowledge assets include all the company's experiences, research, intellectual properties, business models, international know-how, and unique insights harbored within all divisions of the organization. If you are the only one with unique knowledge in an emerging new business, you possess a valuable asset.

Knowledge assets come in multiple forms, including:

» DRIVING CORPORATE EFFICIENCIES BY MINIMIZING OR REINVENTING CURRENT DUPLICATIVE ITEMS
» EMERGING TRENDS IN ANOTHER COUNTRY, SECTOR, OR ALTERNATIVE DISTRIBUTION CHANNELS
» SOCIETAL TRENDS AND THE IMPACT TO THE CURRENT BUSINESS, THE CONSUMER, AND THE INDUSTRY

» EMERGING EFFECTIVE PRACTICES RELATING TO THE INDUSTRY, BUSINESS, PRODUCT, OR SERVICE

» PROPRIETARY TECHNICAL KNOWLEDGE OR RESEARCH UNCOVERS EMERGING CONSUMER NEEDS

» BUSINESS PROCESS IMPROVEMENT THAT THE CUSTOMERS CAN UTILIZE TO IMPROVE THEIR LIVES

GOJO Industries, the creator of PURELL, built a category-defining brand due to their depth of knowledge of the consumer, emerging trends, and formulation superiority.

DIFFERENTIATION THROUGH KNOWLEDGE

From 1996 to 2004, GOJO Industries built a PURELL market share of 70 percent within the U.S., outperforming Colgate's Softsoap, Dial, Unilever's Suave, and Reckitt Benckiser's Lysol.

The PURELL brand was built on tremendous product formulations, unique and portable lifestyle-oriented items, relevant advertising and public relations including outreach to influencers, and deep consumer research.

GOJO Industries had a deep understanding of unmet consumer needs, emerging health care trends, and knowledge of how to bring the hand sanitizer message to health care and governmental influencers.

In 2004, GOJO sold the PURELL consumer brand to Pfizer Consumer Healthcare; later the brand moved over to Johnson & Johnson, which acquired the Pfizer consumer business. Over the next six years, PURELL's consumer market share fell from 70 percent to lower than 20 percent by late 2010. The reason: A dramatic decrease in focus, innovation, specialization, and dedication to insights.

In 2010, GOJO re-acquired PURELL from Johnson & Johnson with the intention of resurrecting the brand with their strongest intangible asset: their depth of knowledge. GOJO uses various professional channels, such as access to hospitals, schools, health clubs, and agencies to undertake experimentation, testing, and prototyping. "The excitement is in discovery," says Joe Kanfer, CEO of GOJO. "I am as excited to find out I'm *wrong* as when I'm right! What was right a year ago can be different a year or two later. The external context changes--which mean the product and your approach must change." [3]

PRODUCT/SERVICE CUSTOMIZATION

Since product or service customization creates complexity, extends resources, and minimizes profitability (at least at first), why would any company want to customize their offering?

If you ask a dark horse company, they will tell you that product or service customization is an *intangible asset* that lets you give your customer a perfect solution. It's a competitive differentiator.

Companies that provide custom solutions meet their customers' needs on a much higher level. This level of customization includes:

» EXCLUSIVE PRODUCTS,
» BUNDLED EXPERIENTIAL ADDED-VALUE ITEMS,
» PERSONALIZED SERVICES,
» TRANSFORMING A PRODUCT, MAKING IT MORE PORTABLE OR PERSONAL, AND
» PRODUCTS THAT ARE CREATED FOR SMALLER, SPECIAL GROUPS
  OF CONSUMERS.

According to most new product research companies, between 80 to 95 percent of all new consumer products fail. Reasons for failure can include not understanding the consumer segment you are speaking to, underestimating your competitors, not effectively communicating what you are offering, not executing your launch plan, or not providing meaningful differentiation from the completion.

The more you can personalize or customize a new product launch, the higher the probability of success and connection with your core consumer. Excellence in customization is the new normal with winning organizations.

NANO-DIFFERENTIATION

We now live in a world of nano-differentiation; there are more solutions than ever before for anything and everything. The problem is that most consumers don't see or appreciate the differences. What do you do with that? Consumers are looking for *real* differentiation, not phantom differentiation. That's where customization enters the picture.

Harvard Professor Youngme Moon, in her book *Different: Escaping the Competitive Herd*, states that at some point the difference between products can become too incremental for even category devotees to appreciate anymore. In other words, there can come a point in the maturation of a category when even the most frequent buyers stop believing the comparative diligence is worth the effort.[4]

Most branded consumer products are not as differentiated in the eyes of consumers as companies would like. This is validated with the rising market share of retailers' private brands and private label offerings. In many health and beauty care categories, the retailers' private brand controls 20 percent to 45 percent of the sales within a category.

Marketers may think they are managing strong brands, but their slipping market shares say otherwise.

CRAYOLA
CUSTOMIZING CREATIVITY

In a world where it seems easy to create knock-off brands, the Crayola crayon company uses design and imagination to deeply connect with the hearts of children and parents. One of Crayola's most powerful hidden assets is their ability to create custom solutions for many of the larger retailers that display their brand.

Prior to the start of each school season, you will find customized Crayola brand products, displays, and advertising programs at key locations in the top traditional and specialty retailers. Crayola understands that the more they can customize solutions that are unique to the retailer, the more valuable they are in the retailer's eyes.

Crayola has licensed their brand name, extending the brand into oral care products, publishing, and Halloween costumes, along with toys and games. Crayola has also partnered with companies such as Mattel with their Hot Wheels and Barbie brands, Disney with Cars and Fairies, and the Warner Brothers characters, Scooby-Doo and Looney Tunes. Crayola is an experiential brand with a distinct personality.

Crayola creates experiences through custom solutions that align with their retail partners, children, and parents (Photos courtesy of Crayola, used with permission. ©2013 Crayola LLC. Crayola Oval Logo, Chevron and Serpentine Designs are registered trademarks of Crayola).

So how can you use customization to better meet the needs of your customers? The following are just a few ideas to get you started:

» PARTNERING WITH ANOTHER LIKE-MINDED ORGANIZATION CREATING A PERSONALIZED SOLUTION FOR THE CONSUMER

» DESIGNING ADDED-VALUE INCENTIVES EXCLUSIVE TO CONSUMER, RETAILER, OR END-USER

» CO-CREATING NEW ITEMS WITH THE CONSUMER AND THE RETAILER

» TESTING EMERGING NEW PRODUCTS WITH A LIMITED GROUP OF CONSUMERS, ONLINE OR WITH A SMALL GROUP OF RETAIL OUTLETS

» MODIFYING A PRODUCT AND ADDING IN NEW EXCLUSIVE ATTRIBUTES FOR A LIMITED PERIOD OF TIME

CONNECTORS

There is usually a particular set of triggers that must occur before a person believes enough in something to move forward with a greater commitment. Each of us has people in our lives that must provide favorable feedback in order for us to feel confident about a decision. These individuals have earned the right to speak in our lives, either because we unquestionably trust them, or they have authority in a topic that we value. In fact, over 75 percent of consumers ask for advice from friends and read product reviews prior to making a purchase decision.

The Great Persuader may be personal experience, but his running mates are influencers we respect. Companies that harness influencers—be they social networks, online influencers, or third-party specialists with retail partners--increase the likelihood of connecting and closing sales. These connectors enable companies to build their brand and their sphere of influence within the industry and with consumers. An organization's connectors (or people of influence) are strong intangibles that can be as valuable as your brand. In fact, it is a valuable part of your brand and a unique asset.

A company's ability to inspire a person with influence to serve as a brand ambassador is an authentic growth strategy. The following are influencer groups that may be hidden within your organization:

» STRATEGIC ALLIANCES, COMPLEMENTARY BRANDS, OR LIKE-MINDED COMPANIES THAT CAN BE ASSOCIATED WITH YOUR BRAND

» SPECIAL INFLUENCERS WHO ARE PART OF YOUR COMPANY OR ARE FRIENDS OF YOUR BRAND

» CREDIBLE COMMUNITIES OF BELIEVERS OR FANS THAT VOLUNTARILY SERVE AS ADVOCATES OF YOUR BRAND

» CO-BRANDING EVENTS AND PROMOTIONS THAT LINK YOUR BRAND TO OTHER BRANDS THAT APPEAL TO THE SAME CONSUMER

» DIRECT MARKETING ENDEAVORS THAT CAN OUTREACH TO YOUR TARGET CONSUMER WITH A SPECIAL, DEEPER EDUCATION OUTREACH

EXPERIENCES

As Youngme Moon writes, "There is a proliferation of sameness rather than differentiation... Products are no longer competing against each other; they are collapsing into each other in the minds of anyone who consumes them." [5] She goes on to state that most companies play a perpetual game of tag with their competitors. One company creates a product, while their competitors run after them and immediately try to copy the idea with very small improvement to the item. The initial creator of the product then returns the favor and starts chasing after the competitor, looking to knock off and improve their product--and so on and so on.

Think of the innumerable kinds of toothpaste on a given supermarket shelf. How many consumers honestly have a passionate preference for a cool mint whitening formula versus cool mint whitening with baking soda? In their effort to keep pace with competitors, manufacturers have flooded stores with far too many variations on the same product; the differences between them are negligible at best and confusing at worst. Companies realize that this phantom differentiation doesn't merit a higher cost—but they ask for it anyway. Consumers seem to know better. A retailer's private label alternative offers roughly the same thing at a much cheaper price. When a name brand can't offer intangibles to sweeten the deal or transform their product, buyers have no problem settling for a less expensive private label alternative.

There is way too much imitation of competitors versus creating meaningful differentiation. Moon states "true differentiation—sustainable differentiation—is rarely a function of well-roundedness; it is typically a function of lopsidedness."[6] True differentiation means you are not afraid of creating consumer experiences that attract your core community and alienate others. Great brands, teams, and organizations create almost a visceral reaction. Sometimes it is positive and often times it is not. But it is distinct.

There are four areas where corporate assets are often hidden: knowledge, product, influencers, and customer experience. Dark horse companies connect with their consumers with brand experiences that are created through:

» TARGETED IN-STORE MARKETING PROGRAMS,
» EXPERIENTIAL MERCHANDISING SYSTEMS AND MEDIA,
» INTERACTIVE EDUCATIONAL KIOSKS,
» COMPREHENSIVE EDUCATION THAT STRENGTHENS RELATIONSHIP WITH THE PRODUCT,
» MARKETING ALLIANCES, AND
» AUTHENTIC ONLINE COMMUNITIES WHICH ENHANCE CONSUMER LOYALTY AND THE COMPANY'S VALUE IN THE EYES OF THE RETAILER AND CONSUMER.

Creating a compelling customer experience has as much to do with *how* you interrupt and engage the consumer as *what* you are engaging Consumer experience is both pragmatic (how something looks and sounds) as well as aesthetic (how it makes you feel). Optimal customer experience attracts, educates, creates connection, and energizes others to become advocates.

YES TO INC.
VERY IMPORTANT CARROTS

Yes To Inc., a line of skin care products made from carrots, tomatoes, and cucumbers, has built a compelling brand based on the initial brand experience at the retailers' shelves. Ido Leffler, co-founder of the San Francisco-based company, introduced the brand exclusively at Walgreens and then extended the brand and their positioning over a three-year window. The company now controls a large portion of the skin care section in many top national retailers.

Yes To had the idea to create a line of natural skin and hair care products that is "guilt-free"—that is, not tested on animals—and formulated with organic fruits and vegetables. When you collide with this brand at retail, you feel the impact and uniqueness. The purity of the product line and the boldness of the colors attract you to the shelf, as does the positivity of the brand name: Yes To.

Yes To Inc. connects with their consumers through experiential product formulas, packaging, and a strong brand image at the shelf level.

When I spoke with Leffler, he shared his love for the brand: "When we started this company we wanted to make a difference in the culture—mainstreaming natural products. We weren't looking to create a set of products for the natural consumer only; we wanted to design products that met the natural consumers' approval—but bridge to new users.

"What was our vision? We wanted to make something that was accessible—sexy, beautiful—and something that others can get connected to. As consumers, we couldn't find brands that met our personal natural beauty needs, so we focused on creating products that blended efficacy, style, and affordability. We create products for a very special group of zealous consumers who we have named VICs, or Very Important Carrots. They love the brand and our commitment to creating clean, fun products."

Leffler says, "Our consumer target is referred to as the Yes To Stylista. These are fans of ours who love to be stylish, but embrace natural products which are good for you. We aggressively used all facets of social media to build one-on-one relationships with our core consumers. Even though we have only been a company since 2006, we are currently one of the highest ranked beauty brands in Facebook interactions."[7]

In a world where we are over-stimulated with marketing messages, the Yes To design and colors compels us to take a second look at the offering. The company's ability to create a personal experience, within a larger category of products, is indeed an inspiring hidden asset.

Here are some potential approaches to creating a stronger brand experience:

- » CREATE IN-STORE EDUCATION EVENTS AND/OR ONLINE CUSTOMER EXPERIENCES THAT DEMONSTRATE YOU UNDERSTAND CUSTOMERS' LIVES AND PERSONAL NEEDS.
- » CO-BRAND WITH COMPLEMENTARY BRANDS TO CREATE A DEEPER RELATIONSHIP WITH YOUR CONSUMER.
- » INTRODUCE CUSTOMERS AND INFLUENCERS TO OTHER LIKE-MINDED ORGANIZATIONS WHO HAVE THE SAME VALUES, NEEDS, AND ASPIRATIONS.
- » INTRODUCE INFLUENCERS TO YOUR MOST TRUSTED CUSTOMERS.

DENTEK ORAL CARE
TRUSTED ADVISOR TO RETAILERS

How do you compete for space, relevance, and share of mind against some of the largest oral-care companies in world?

DenTek Oral Care Inc. is a dark horse company that designs unique oral-care products sold in retail stores around the world. In 1984, a twenty-one-year-old entrepreneur named John Jansheski founded the company in Northern California. John and his father created an at-home tartar removal dental pick that was accepted by a small group of California drugstores and eventually brought to the retail masses. The company has created a wide variety of specialized oral-care products that address teeth cleaning and flossing, and accessories such as teeth grinding innovations.

A lot of design and passion goes into an effective floss pick...

Just ask DenTek.

In 2001 Jansheski moved the company to a small town outside of Knoxville, Tennessee, and built a portfolio of oral health items that, on store shelves, are next to the likes of Johnson & Johnson, Colgate, and Proctor & Gamble in the interdental/flossing accessories oral care section.

Oral care is big business. Most companies have a difficult time staying in business due to the aggressive expansion plans of Proctor & Gamble and Colgate. So how does DenTek stay relevant and keep growing?

Very few companies understand the broader consumer megatrends relating to their category. This is where DenTek provides a unique hidden asset to their consumers and the retailers that shelve their products. DenTek offers third-party advisory support; they supply trend data and insights in oral care categories that they do *not* play in. Essentially, they validate what the other top oral-care companies are saying about emerging trends and winning practices with other competing retailers. They serve the role of trusted advisor because they have nothing to gain from their feedback; they serve an objective role in many retailers' eyes.

Lex Shankle, who led the marketing and brand experience for DenTek from 2001 to 2011, says, "Our secret weapon was speed to market, flexibility, and agility, deep understanding of the retailer's larger needs, and trust. We provided insights and benchmarks with most portions of the oral care company, whether we played in this part of the category or not. Our vision was to truly serve as third-party resources helping our partners understand the truth of the broader category. After a while *our retail partners knew we were looking out for them*, not ourselves. And that was unique, or so we were told."[8]

INTANGIBLES CREATE DIFFERENTIATION

Some dark horse companies create competitive differentiation not by what they make, but by

» THEIR REPUTATION AS THINKERS,
» THEIR INSIGHTS INTO EMERGING CONSUMERS,
» THE COMMUNITIES THEY NURTURE,
» THE AGILITY OF THEIR CULTURE,
» THEIR KNOW-HOW IN FIXING PROBLEMS, AND
» THE HUMAN CAPITAL WITHIN THEIR TEAMS.

Whether it is the sales team, marketing staff, customer service department, or manufacturing groups, everyone must be uncovering new assets and competitive insights, and be creating ideas or solving problems in ways that create value for their customers.

WHAT UNIQUE **HIDDEN ASSETS** ARE STORED AWAY IN **YOUR** CORPORATE CUPBOARD?

INSIGHTS ON HIDDEN ASSETS

» COMPANIES AND BRANDS ARE MADE UP OF IMPRESSIONS, INSIGHTS, IDEAS, AND INTANGIBLES.

» IT'S VITAL TO STOCKPILE AND PROTECT RELEVANT INTELLECTUAL PROPERTIES SINCE WE NOW LIVE IN AN ECONOMY WHERE EVERYTHING CAN BE COPIED. EVERYTHING IS UP FOR GRABS.

» DARK HORSE COMPANIES *WIN WITH IDEAS*. YOUR COMPANY'S IDEAS MAY BE MORE VALUABLE THAN YOUR PRODUCTS.

» DARK HORSES SET THE RULES OF ENGAGEMENT AND ARE OPINION LEADERS TO CUSTOMERS AND INFLUENCERS THAT SUPPORT THEIR ORGANIZATION.

» MOST NEW ITEM VENTURES FAIL BECAUSE OF LACK OF BRAND AWARENESS, UNDERESTIMATING COMPETITORS, LACK OF TRUE DIFFERENTIATION, OR SIMPLY NOT EXECUTING THE ORIGINAL PLAN.

» TANGIBLE PRODUCTS PROVIDE EXPECTED VALUE, WHILE INTANGIBLES (IDEAS) CAN UNLEASH BUSINESS TRANSFORMATION.

» THERE IS A PROLIFERATION OF PRODUCT SAMENESS RATHER THAN DIFFERENTIATION. DON'T BE AFRAID TO CREATE PRODUCTS THAT ATTRACT YOUR CORE CONSUMERS AND ALIENATE OTHERS.

» CORPORATE ASSETS ARE MOST OFTEN HIDDEN IN KNOWLEDGE, PRODUCT CUSTOMIZATION, CONNECTORS, AND EXPERIENCES.

THOUGHT STARTERS

1. HOW CAN YOU CUSTOMIZE YOUR PRODUCT OFFERING FOR YOUR TOP CUSTOMERS?

2. WHAT IS THE NEXT GENERATION OF INNOVATION YOU MUST CREATE TO STAY AHEAD OF YOUR COMPETITORS?

3. WHAT UNIQUE INSIGHT OR SKILL LIES WITHIN ANOTHER DIVISION OR DEPARTMENT IN YOUR COMPANY?

4. WHAT UNIQUE PEOPLE OR INFLUENCERS DO YOU KNOW, AND HOW DO YOU UTILIZE THESE PEOPLE TO CREATE A DEEPER RELATIONSHIP WITH YOUR TOP CUSTOMERS?

5. DO YOU UNDERSTAND YOUR CUSTOMERS AND HAVE YOU INVESTED IN INFORMAL RESEARCH TO VALIDATE THEIR IMPRESSIONS OF YOU?

6. DO YOU SPEND TIME EACH WEEK HANGING OUT IN DIFFERENT VENUES LOOKING FOR NON-RELATED IDEAS THAT MAY IMPROVE YOUR OPERATION?

7. DO YOU HAVE ENOUGH ALTERNATIVE THINKERS ON YOUR TEAM? ARE YOU GOING OUT AND HIRING SOME?

8. WHAT ARE THE INTANGIBLES THAT YOU BRING TO YOUR CUSTOMER RELATIONSHIPS, AND HOW DO YOU KNOW THAT THESE INTANGIBLES ARE VALUABLE TO CUSTOMERS?

Chapter 4:

THE VITAL FEW (CHOOSE YOUR CUSTOMERS WISELY)

Never mistake motion for action.

—ERNEST HEMINGWAY, NOVELIST

Just because a customer creates a lot of activity—phone calls, emails, or visits—doesn't mean they are necessarily providing value. Research shows that the top 20 percent of customers contribute 150 percent of the average company's profits, while the bottom 20 percent drains profits by at least 80 percent. And here's the kicker: these customers will more than likely *remain* unprofitable unless a different sales model is put in place.[1]

Most organizations don't have the courage or discipline to radically commit to their most valuable customers, the ones who will deliver the most long term value. Let's face it; it takes nerve to commit to a smaller group of customers, trusting that when you increase your intimacy with them, you will create more revenue than broadening your base to a more transactional group of customers. It seems like an easy choice, but very few organizations fully commit to this customer segmentation model because they don't believe they can create enough value to warrant the decision. *But not dark horse organizations; many of them go deeper with fewer customers.*

It is not a surprise that the best brands and leaders don't appeal or cater to the masses. Many of the most unique companies we have researched choose a customer segment and make a pact with them, committing to not violate their trust. In other words, they choose their customers wisely and go all in with fewer customers, understanding the power of clarity and the value of dedicating themselves to a smaller group of consumers. They fully commit to the idea that 20 percent of their customers (their vital few) have the potential to create 80 percent of their revenue. By committing to fewer customers, they create deeper, stronger and more profitable relationships.

Top-performing dark horse companies do not treat all their customers the same; they support them based on the value they bring to their organization. They go deeper with their vital few top customers, while either eliminating or managing more effectively the unprofitable and demanding customers. Smaller companies have limited capital and human resources, and a good first step is setting a clear line of demarcation between who your customers are and who they are not. It may be one of the most significant decisions your business makes!

DISCIPLINED CUSTOMER SEGMENTATION

How do you partner with your best customers while providing all your customers with an honest product or service? The answer is reflected in how you segment and assign an overall value or role to each of them. Disciplined customer segmentation allows you to focus on the subset that is more profitable and loyal to ensure the highest return on your investments. Your most valuable customers must be protected, listened to, cultivated, and inspired to become influencers of your business. It is a smart approach to focus your thinking, resources, and strategy on customers who

» HAVE THE STRONGEST GROWTH POTENTIAL AND ARE PROFITABLE;

» ARE PERSONALLY ALIGNED WITH YOUR PRODUCT AND ARE LOYAL;

» HAVE INFLUENCE AND ARE WILLING TO TELL OTHERS ABOUT YOU;

» ARE WILLING TO PROVIDE FEEDBACK THAT HELPS IMPROVE THE QUALITY OF YOUR PRODUCTS; AND

» ARE IN A LONG-STANDING RELATIONSHIP WITH YOU AND WANT TO CONTINUE THE PARTNERSHIP.

Historically, customer segmentation was simply a measure of the sales or profit generated by each customer, listing them in the descending order of size. However, these only measure the *quantitative value* of the customer portfolio, not the *intangible value*—that is, the potential value, the loyalty, or the long-term role of a customer. Just like hidden assets, as discussed in the last chapter, intangibles count for a lot when it comes to customer selection.

A new customer model is bubbling up that focuses on a broader, more strategic set of criteria for customers. Dark horse companies often use this model, valuing other aspects besides size and the scale of the customer. They consider five key criteria:

ALIGNMENT—Does your brand essence match up with the customers' image of themselves? If the answer is "yes," the stronger the alignment potential, and the stronger the attachment and loyalty factors.

INNOVATION—Not all customers are passionate or skilled at providing your company with the valuable insight you need to compete now and in the future. Many dark horse companies create a covenant relationship with their most zealous consumers. Even smaller customers who are not financially significant are strategically important if they are early adopters of your products and are invested in your innovation processes.

ADVOCACY—Customers willing to serve as societal influencers or evangelists of your brand are vital to your organization's growth and image. Even if their buying power is small, customers who have passion for sharing their love of your company deserve your time and your ear.

MAINTAINABILITY—Not all sales have long-term potential, and not all customers are interested in long-term relationships. One of the strongest corporate skills is to have the clarity and poise to not invest in customer relationships that are not maintainable. Cash flow is always king, but strategically positioned companies invest their most valuable asset—their time—with customers who are with them for the long haul.

PROFITABILITY—A key determinate of a customer's role in your portfolio should be the actual net profit delivered by the customer throughout the year in relation to the overhead and time invested to earn this business.

If a customer performs well in each of these criteria, they are very valuable to the long term health of your business. Each of these five criteria allows a company to create a balanced customer scorecard, which can help minimize risk, plan for the future, grow profitability, and partner with your top customers.

Many entrepreneurial organizations are attracted to shiny things—big new clients with the potential for immediate new revenue and profit—but this is not sustainable, and often times not profitable. Shiny things are too good to be true. On the other hand, customers of high value can come in many colors, textures, and sizes; what they have in common is loyalty, profitability, and connectedness to your brand.

Wal-Mart, Target, CVS, Rite Aid, and Walgreens are very valuable to any marketer of beauty brands; all five retailers have great

the best dark horse companies utilize a balanced scorecard in evaluating and grouping their top customers.

WINNING
WITH
THE "FEW"

societal influence. But influential retailers come in all sizes and shapes. Boutique specialty or regional operators—such as Giant Eagle in Pittsburgh, H-E-B in San Antonio, Ulta Beauty in Chicago, and Wegmans in Rochester New York—provide their own value and their own form of influence. Many times they offer their stores as laboratories in which companies can test their products or invent new consumer solutions. Scale is important to delivering today's business plan, but smaller retailers with influence and insight are just as valuable to creating the future.

CAN YOU SAY "NO" TO A CUSTOMER?

The courage to say "no" or to de-emphasize a customer's role in your company is a vital management skill. All customers contribute value, but have different roles, and the energy deployed must be commensurate to the value created. We find that most companies struggle with this management discipline. But how organizations spend time with their *least valuable* customers is a key indicator of how successful they will be with their *more valuable* customers.

A CUSTOMER SEGMENTATION METHODOLOGY

The following is a segmentation methodology that we have noticed many dark horse companies informally using as they manage their customer portfolio more effectively. It is broken up into

» VITAL CUSTOMERS
» DRIVE CUSTOMERS
» VALUE CUSTOMERS

THE VITAL CUSTOMER

Vital customers are the foundation of your company: though normally less than 10-20 percent of customers, they account for more than 60 percent of revenue. Due to their enormous value, there is an inherent benefit in having the whole organization thinking about these customers, serving their needs, and evaluating future unstated needs. We have found that these customers deserve a larger share of mind, and are, unfortunately, often under-developed. What should your team be thinking about?

» INTIMATELY DEVELOP PLANS THAT ALIGN WITH CUSTOMERS' VISION AND MINIMIZE THEIR VULNERABILITIES.
» UNDERSTAND WHAT "VALUE" MEANS TO THEM.
» GAIN A RICH UNDERSTANDING OF THEIR UNSTATED NEEDS.
» FOCUS ON BREAKTHROUGH RELATIONSHIP MANAGEMENT STRATEGIES.
» DECIPHER THE ROLE OF CULTURAL TRENDS IN THEIR LIVES.
» ENSURE THAT YOUR BRAND DRAMATICALLY OUTPERFORMS ALL FINANCIAL REQUIREMENTS.
» COMPREHEND THEIR DREAMS AND ASPIRATIONS.

As I've learned in my research and consulting work, if you don't delight these high-profile, loyal customers, you will more than likely see yourself displaced—especially if any of your competitors are dark horses! My Elevation Forum executive group—a team of dark horses if ever there was one—knows that I'll do almost anything to protect and nurture my core clients. Winning companies understand that being faithful to vital customers inspires deeper loyalty and a halo effect with all customers.

This idea of optimizing business impact through clear customer segmentation is one of the disciplines that make Target so special. This retailer doesn't try to be all things to all people; they purposefully market their business to young mothers, younger singles, and empty nesters who appreciate the retailer's cheap chic image. It is estimated that 15 percent of Target's core consumers deliver more than half of the retailer's revenue.

Influencer customers are attracted to the image of the company and actively purchase a number of the company's exclusive brands by designers such as Mossimo, Michael Graves, Isaac Mizrahi, and Amy Coe. Target has used these brands to insulate itself against competition and has earned loyalty in the minds of their guests. Target understands

Duane Reade's high-profile 40 Wall Street store is positioned and marketed towards the business community and consumers in this affluent Manhattan neighborhood.

that these few private brands make a huge difference to their vital customers.

Other retailers have moved dramatically in this direction, including CVS Caremark, Rite Aid, Kroger, Walgreens, Safeway, and New York's Duane Reade drugstore (which is owned by Walgreens). Each of these drugstores have taken a page out of the Target playbook, but instead of bringing in proprietary designers, architects, and artists, they have redesigned a wide portfolio of private brands that are exclusive to their four walls and that delight their core consumers. The Duane Reade store on 40 Wall Street in Manhattan screams experience; its upscale, boutique feel is tailored to the needs and lifestyle of the neighborhood. This Wall Street drugstore provides higher-end food, beauty, and cosmetic products specifically for their most valuable vital consumers.

Vital customers are essential to your business, core to your growth, and they serve the role of evangelist for your company. Oh, and did I mention that vital customers are the people who won't leave you because of a slight price increase?

THE DRIVE CUSTOMER

Drive customers are the heart of your business (the majority of your customers) even though they do not hold down the lion's share of a company's sales. These customers deliver consistent revenue and have a strong sense of loyalty, but they do not individually constitute the largest sales contribution, nor do they carry societal influence.

As a group, this customer segment provides a steady stream of profitable revenue. We have found that there is great value in setting up discovery time with drive customers to better understand how you are serving them and to help uncover your performance blind spots. However, invest your time wisely with this group and keep in mind their limited growth potential. The service goal with drive customers is to maintain a strong leadership position without wasting valuable time or resources. It is necessary to collaborate with the customer, but it is just as important to know when enough is enough. At some point in all service relationships, companies need to focus on giving the customer what they want, not what you think they want.

It is necessary to understand the following questions with drive customers:

» WHO ELSE PROVIDES A SIMILAR SERVICE IN THEIR EYES?
» WHAT ARE THEIR CHANGING NEEDS, AND WHY ARE THEY CHANGING?
» WHAT ELSE DO THEY SEE OR EXPERIENCE THAT DELIGHTS THEM?
» HOW DO YOUR COMPETITORS INFLUENCE THEM?
» DO THEY BELIEVE YOUR COMPANY IS PROVIDING VALUE?

Drive customers are the core of your business. This valuable group of customers, and how they see you, is often a strong reflection of your corporate health and the value of your proposition. They are a great group of customers to ask, "How am I doing, and what's next?" Their impression is a good barometer of how others perceive you.

THE VALUE CUSTOMER

Value customers are small in size, many in number, and are often higher maintenance. Before you rush to eliminate them and move to larger, more profitable customers, know that they have the potential to offer value *if they are managed appropriately.*

Since value customers can be pulled away from your business by a more competitive price at any moment, how you service them still matters. The goal is *not* to go deep with them, but to meet their basic needs profitably. You should be thinking through how you use technology or other variables—such as offering no-frills products and services—to meet their transactional needs. Uncover their basic needs by asking value customers three simple questions:

» WHAT KEEPS YOU COMING BACK FOR MORE?
» WHAT WOULD MAKE YOU LEAVE OR NOT COME BACK?
» HOW CAN WE MAKE YOU HAPPY?

By all means, de-emphasize the value customers so you can focus on the winning few customers. Perfectionists have to accept that in some instances, perfection isn't necessary with value customers; save that extra effort for your more valuable consumers. Are you creating the next generation of innovation with these influencers?

Let Meijer show you how.

MEIJER INC.
UNDERSTANDING CUSTOMERS ONE NEIGHBORHOOD AT A TIME

Meijer Inc., the mass-discount chain from Michigan, is a Midwestern regional powerhouse that deeply understands the communities they serve. Growing slowly, thoughtfully, and profitably for decades, Meijer sells grocery items, general merchandise, clothing, house supplies, wines, and fresh foods. The following story exemplifies their winning strategy of understanding their vital customers and dominating the selective markets they operate in.

Meijer first ventured into the Chicago area in 1999 with a store in Bolingbrook, Illinois; this early venture didn't go smoothly because they didn't understand the local tastes of people in Chicago. So Meijer slowed its Chicago-area expansion for a decade, then took another swing at this market during the price-sensitive recession. Prior to the 2011 store opening in Melrose Park—an outlying suburb of Chicago—the Meijer team of merchandisers spent weeks visiting stores within a three-mile radius to find out what the neighborhood was missing.

Meijer employees pride themselves on understanding their customers' household needs: how they shop and, more importantly, how they cook and prepare their food. "Chicago is very different from

Grand Rapids," says Laurie Wharton, Meijer's VP of Merchandising and Marketing in Chicago. "It's up to us to tell Meijer headquarters what those differences are." [2]

This vibrant organization has been winning with the few for decades through controlled growth, outreach to vital customers, understanding local markets, and dedication to making a difference in these local markets. Meijer pays attention to each unique neighborhood they serve and has created a unique brand that delivers extreme value, experience, and intimate customer service. That trifecta is difficult to beat.

When the economy fell in 2008 and most retailers got rid of secondary items in their stores to improve efficiency, Meijer didn't. They maintained the broadest variety of products in the grocery industry. That's because they understood that their vital customers want variety as much as they want great prices and convenience. (Actually, that strategy appealed to all three types of customers: vital, drive, and value customers!) As a result, Meijer's customer base has steadily grown throughout the recession and alongside daunting competition.

CARMA LABS INC.
LOVED BY TRUSTED PARTNERS

After decades of lip care leadership, Carma Labs has now extended beyond Carmex lip balm into lotions and creams.

Carma Labs Inc. is a company with a loyal group of consumer zealots who don't leave home without their Carmex lip balm. This family-owned company has been making lip treatment products since the 1930s. Their formula is the topic of great debate on the internet, and their followers are as passionate as they come.

To get to the next level of business success, Carma Labs decided to partner with major retailer Walgreens. Carmex Healing Lotion was initially launched at this retailer; the launch strategy was very conservative and highly focused on testing the concept in the real world—but *only at Walgreens.* [3]

Since Carma Labs wanted to minimize risk on their new venture into lotions, they chose a retail partner that had been a company advocate and influencer for decades. It was also very helpful that the sales and marketing departments of Carma Labs are within driving distance of the Walgreens headquarters.

There are many examples of dark horse companies that have partnered successfully with major retailers:

» AVENT NURSING AND PREMIUM BABY PRODUCTS USED A SIMILAR INNOVATION AND CREATION STRATEGY WITH TARGET PRIOR TO BEING ACQUIRED BY PHILIPS.
» YES TO INC. PARTNERS WITH WALGREENS.
» DENTEK ORAL CARE PARTNERS WITH WAL-MART AND TARGET.
» GOJO INDUSTRIES PARTNERS WITH TARGET.
» WAHL HOME PRODUCTS PARTNERS WITH WAL-MART AND WALGREENS
» SUNSTAR AMERICA'S PARTNERS WITH WALGREENS.

What are the advantages of using this retail partnership approach? The risk of large-scale financial failure is reduced while collaborating with the retailer and using their brand-building awareness programs to market to consumers. The largest retailers are often more than willing to offer higher-impact advertising programs when a manufacturer chooses to partner with them on a new brand or item.

What are the challenges with a limited retail launch? There is always the risk of alienating other valuable retail partners with a limited retail launch; however, dark horse companies do not alienate themselves from other retailers. They may offer alternative products to test with other national retailer partners, and they are always committed to open communication with everyone. Their transparency and integrity is vital to ensuring that everyone is aware of new products that are in test or limited launch mode.

METHOD
DESIGN FOCUS SUITS TARGET

Method, the Northern California soap maker introduced in the first chapter, enjoys national distribution at all of the top retailers; however,

Target, one of their early partners, was vital to building their identity and presence across the country. "Target got us early in the game," says Method co-founder Eric Ryan. "They felt our vision and commitment to them and were supportive of our creative culture and our obsessions of speed to market, consumer experience, creating advocates, product design, and making cleaning fun."

George Shumny, Method's Vice President of Sales during the growth years, notes that Method is first and foremost a design firm that makes soap and home products, not a manufacturer who does great design—and this description fits Target like a glove. "It really was an upside down model," recalls Shumny. "Method outsourced the disciplines that most package goods companies keep in house. The most important assets of the brand were nurtured internally, including design, fragrance, formulation, and improved product sustainability. This positioned us as unique in our partner's eyes. The costs to support these departments were substantial, but we were committed to these pillars. This is typically unheard of for a startup and even a company of this size."

During one of their first meetings with Target, the Method team noticed that going through the traditional buying channels—the merchandising and purchasing departments—was not working. In true Method form, the team turned and went through Target's marketing department. They also partnered with world-renowned designer Karim Rashid on the initial product design, which helped set the stage for their brand imagery and corporate essence.

Method was founded on zero paid ads, yet they built an iconic brand through the groundswell of earned or influencer advertising. George Shumny says that Method had to constantly strive to be different from their competitors in the marketplace. "We had a poster in our office that asked 'What Would P&G Do?' to remind us that we would likely have to do the opposite. We realized we could never 'out-Procter Procter'. We just didn't have that type of traditional marketing muscle." Method's market share is growing, but what's growing even faster is the loyalty of their followers and customers. [4]

PICK YOUR CUSTOMERS WISELY

Dark horse companies get more sales and profit out of their top customers because they do not waste valuable thinking and energy on lower-value customers. In other words, they treat all customers fairly, but spend less time and resources with the lower-worth customers.

The benefits of a disciplined customer segmentation strategy that focuses on the "valuable few" customers that create the most value include: stronger positioning versus larger competitors, improved clarity around what really matters, increased customer retention, and improved productivity and morale.

In a hyper-competitive world, you must get more out of your higher potential customers. This demands a precise and disciplined customer segmentation and management strategy.

How are you evaluating and managing your customer base?

INSIGHTS ON WINNING WITH FEW

» THE TOP 20 PERCENT OF CUSTOMERS CONTRIBUTE 150 PERCENT OF PROFITS. THE BOTTOM 20 PERCENT DRAIN PROFITS BY AT LEAST 80 PERCENT.

» DARK HORSE COMPANIES DON'T TREAT ALL CUSTOMERS THE SAME; THEY SUPPORT THEM BASED ON THE VALUE THEY BRING TO THEIR ORGANIZATION. THEY GO DEEPER WITH FEWER CUSTOMERS.

» WITH BOTTOM CUSTOMERS, MANAGE DIFFERENTLY, IMPROVE PROFITABILITY, OR GET RID OF THEM.

» YOUR MOST VALUABLE CUSTOMERS MUST BE PROTECTED, LISTENED TO, CULTIVATED AND INSPIRED TO BECOME INFLUENCERS OF YOUR BUSINESS.

» ALL CUSTOMERS CONTRIBUTE VALUE, BUT HAVE DIFFERENT ROLES, AND THE ENERGY DEPLOYED MUST BE COMMENSURATE TO THE VALUE CREATED.

» HOW ORGANIZATIONS SPEND TIME WITH THEIR *LEAST VALUABLE* CUSTOMERS IS A KEY INDICATOR OF HOW SUCCESSFUL THEY WILL BE WITH THEIR *MORE VALUABLE* CUSTOMERS.

» THE *RIGHT* CUSTOMERS ARE THOSE WHO SHARE IDEAS, ADVOCATE FOR YOUR BRAND, HAVE STAYING POWER, AND ARE PROFITABLE.

THOUGHT STARTERS

1. HOW DO YOU SEGMENT OR ASSIGN VALUE TO YOUR CUSTOMERS MORE EFFECTIVELY?

2. ARE YOU SPENDING YOUR TIME CULTIVATING THE MOST VALUABLE CUSTOMERS?

3. WHICH CUSTOMERS HAVE SOCIETAL INFLUENCE, AND HOW DO YOU LEVERAGE THEIR INFLUENCE?

4. WHICH HIGH-POTENTIAL CUSTOMERS ARE UNDERPERFORMING AND WHICH CUSTOMERS NEED ADDITIONAL RESOURCES?

5. WHICH CUSTOMERS ARE UNPROFITABLE BASED ON REVENUE-TO-TIME INVESTED AND HOW DO YOU REDUCE YOUR TIME COMMITMENT WHILE MAINTAINING THE REVENUE?

6. DO YOUR MOST VALUABLE CUSTOMERS RECEIVE THE LION'S SHARE OF YOUR COMPANY'S TIME AND RESOURCES, SUCH AS YOUR MOST TALENTED EMPLOYEES? IF NOT, WHY NOT?

7. HOW CAN YOU NARROW YOUR FOCUS AND CREATE EVEN MORE VALUE WITH YOUR MOST VALUABLE CUSTOMERS?

8. ARE THERE EMERGING CUSTOMERS WHO MAY BE SMALL TODAY, BUT VALUABLE IN THE FUTURE?

Chapter 5:

CO-CREATION

Inventing the Future

The best way to predict the future is to invent it.

—ALAN KAY, COMPUTER SCIENTIST

Products are no longer created; they are co-created. In fact, controlling your innovation or customer service process is certainly a recipe for underperformance, and potentially a recipe for failure. Are you risking co-creating the future with your top customers?

The rules of engagement are changing right before our eyes: limited loyalty, scarce capital, and a dramatic reduction in consumer spending have created a new business landscape. These trends provide a unique opportunity for agile, innovative, and insightful companies to improve their customer alignment, sales growth, and the quality of their client relations.

This new economy is being shaped by an emerging strategy known as *customer co-creation*. Co-creation is the process of listening deeply to customers and all stakeholders while working together to design new or deeper consumer solutions that address new or unmet needs. This strategy is repositioning how manufacturers are relating to their customers when designing new products; it is transforming how business is done altogether. In the past, the consumer's voice was a component of the new product process, but today the consumer and all stakeholders have a voice in the innovation process. The process is very fluid and is no longer passive.

Why is co-creation important? Because it helps organizations answer the most important question lying at their feet: "If your organization where to close your doors today, would anyone care?" Co-creation creates care, and care creates authenticity, relevance, and the opportunity to thrive. A culture that embraces co-creation embraces transparency with all stakeholders and allows the freedom to have risky, honest conversations. It gives you the permission to go places and talk about ideas that most teams never address, due to political, individual, or corporate pressure. Co-creation is a true growth enabler!

As one higher level buyer once shared with me, "Too often sales and marketing leaders are rigid and sound like they are working off of a script. The best sales and service companies visit me *before* they are ready to present a new product. Prior to selling me something, they inquire into my unmet needs, their competitors, and ask me questions pertaining to emerging new ideas that may relate to their business." The buyer reminded me that the best sales and service organizations have an outward focus and are constantly in a state of diagnosing and reviewing the changing dynamics all around their business.

The rules of higher level partnerships are changing. Today's partnerships include transparent storytelling, where both parties are invited to join the other's story. They then co-create the solution together, gaining the best out of each other's hidden assets and insights.

If you are not interactively co-creating future products and solutions with your top customers, you have an alignment gap.

MYSTARBUCKSIDEA.COM
CONSUMERS PITCH IN WITH IDEAS

During the economic downfall of 2008, Starbucks—the darling of American industry for a decade—hit the floor. As the economy went into free fall and the value consumer became king, Starbucks found itself over-retailed and out of sync with the new frugal customer.

Starbucks CEO Howard Schultz, known as a relentless experience guy, relied on one of his strengths: deep listening to his customers, employees, and critics. He launched MyStarbucksIdea.com and encouraged his consumers to co-create the future with his company.

In the first year—2008—a total of 65,000 ideas were submitted, and by the end of 2009, more than fifty ideas had been approved by Starbucks and incorporated into their operation. This included Free Coffee on Your Birthday, Gluten Free Packaged Foods, Happy Hour, an iPhone app, and Darker Chocolate Mocha.[1]

During one of the largest crises in the company's history, Starbucks relied on co-creation to help reposition the ship.

Co-creation is an open business culture that emphasizes an outward focus of listening, generating ideas with customers, and evaluating ideas that may be bubbling up on the fringes of your industry. This philosophy views customers as validators of the next generation of innovation and as a source for innovation. The best co-created solutions are very personal experiences that reflect the needs of the consumer or end user.

Essentially, the consumers' fingerprints are all over the process; the resulting new product or service embodies the consumer's identity and is something the consumer personally brands. They are loyal to the product because they helped create it.

We see these trends emerging in all facets of the economy, whether it is in Nike's custom shoes, ladies' handbags, the digital music industry, or in any market that allows for a personalized customer experience. The more a consumer voice is reflected in the design of a product, and the more personalized the product experience, the more co-creation was utilized in the development process.

WHAT IS THE MARKETING BENEFIT OF CO-CREATION?

Companies that possess a much deeper understanding of their customers' needs create stronger loyalty and advocacy with these customers, and they create a community of believers that help lead and guide the innovation process. Consumers and retailers who buy and sell products need to be able to voice their opinions and share their insights; they are invaluable in creating consumer and brand alignment.

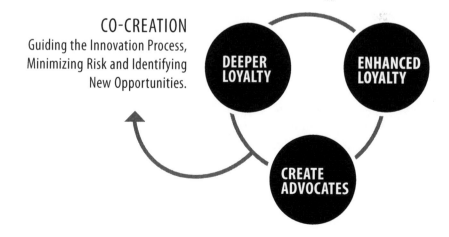

CO-CREATION
Guiding the Innovation Process, Minimizing Risk and Identifying New Opportunities.

DEEPER LOYALTY

ENHANCED LOYALTY

CREATE ADVOCATES

The idea of co-creation and innovation has been used, informally, by small business owners and entrepreneurs since the beginning of time. Intuitive business people have always known that the best way to sell something is to go to the consumer, ask them what they want, and then make it for them.

ARE YOU CREATING A NEW PRODUCT JUST TO FILL SHELF SPACE?

But that rather obvious idea gets lost at many larger companies who often create products without fully appreciating the consumer's stated or unstated needs. The criticism is that they create new products just because they need something to recapture lost shelf space.

Formal market research and face-to-face co-creation are running mates, and the best dark horse companies run with both philosophies. Optimal innovation and execution occurs when they are both operating synergistically together.

Dark horse companies are adept at creating the next generation of innovation; they possess cultural and societal insights that do not always show up in focus groups, allowing them the advantage of creating products that fill consumer whitespaces or needs currently not being addressed on the shelf. In other words, they know things others don't know, allowing them the insight to design solutions that others haven't imagined, due to emerging consumer needs or the effects of new technologies.

BUILD A *DIFFERENT* MOUSETRAP

Neil Rackham, author and founder of the sales consulting company Huthwaite Inc., states that "Twenty years ago you could argue quite plausibly that the value you provided to customers largely rested in your products… but today, customers have many mousetraps to choose from; as far as they are concerned, your mousetrap might have some unique features, but so do ten competing mousetraps. You may have differentiated your product, but the differentiation does not create value because it doesn't *matter* to the customer." [2]

In a world of sameness, dark horse firms use co-creation discussions with their top customers to unleash intangible assets (knowledge, insights, alternative views), and allow the team to create products that are better than their competitors. The co-creation process can unearth

» NEW PACKAGING,
» CO-BRANDING IDEAS,
» ADDED VALUE SERVICES, AND
» ALLIANCE PARTNERS.

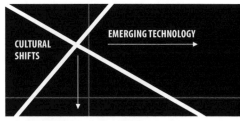

Ideas Emerge at the Intersection of Cultural Shifts & Emerging Technologies

If your product is not the key differentiator, then your knowledge better be unique!

TIPS FOR A GREAT CO-CREATION PROCESS

1. Sit down and listen to customers, influencers, innovators, bloggers—any thinkers who are on the edge of movements surrounding the product.

2. The best co-creation discussions include a diverse group of consumers who are comfortable providing blunt, insightful understandings into their unmet needs.

3. If you want to birth ideas, you must engage people *who don't think like you.*

4. Co-creation innovation is optimized in informal small groups, allowing for energetic banter, dissension, and critique of ideas.

5. The best co-creation occurs when the manufacturer serves as facilitator, listening to what is both stated and not stated by the customer.

6. Great co-creation includes designers, marketers, sales, senior leadership, and multiple customers. The leaders must have face-to-face experiences with the end-user.

7. The best co-creation meetings are high on show and tell, personal stories, insights, photographs, images, and they appeal to the consumer's personal life and experience. This is accomplished through sharing new ideas, sketches, prototypes, and any other tool that creates emotion.

GOJO INDUSTRIES
CO-CREATING INFLUENCER MARKETING PROGRAMS

When I worked at GOJO Industries—the creator of PURELL instant hand sanitizer—I was privileged to facilitate several co-creation meetings with the top retail customers and zealous consumers. Both consumers and retailers helped guide the design of many of the influencer marketing programs that introduced the brand to many future loyal consumers. The ideas that came out of these rooms ended up being pivotal to carving a 70 percent market share for PURELL in the beginning stages of brand development. Upon witnessing this, I was struck by the notion that *this is how effective business ought to be done*, as these meetings produced novel ideas we could not have arrived at otherwise. Those ideas were as follows:

» THE CREATION OF A SCHOLASTIC TEACHER'S EDUCATIONAL CURRICULUM ENTITLED *HANDS-ON LEARNING: READING AND WRITING AT HOME*, MADE AVAILABLE TO TEACHERS WHO WISHED TO EDUCATE KIDS ON EFFECTIVE HAND HYGIENE.

» A LIVE PHARMACY EDUCATIONAL TRAINING SIMULCAST THAT EDUCATED AND INFLUENCED THE NATIONAL RETAILER'S PHARMACY COMMUNITY ABOUT STAYING HEALTHY BY USING A HAND SANITIZER MULTIPLE TIMES PER DAY WHILE SERVING CONSUMERS AT THE PHARMACY DESK.

» A DAYCARE PROVIDER MARKETING OUTREACH PROGRAM, DEVELOPED FOR AND CO-BRANDED WITH A NATIONAL RETAILER.[3]

What are the steps for successful co-creation? Let's take a look.

THE CO-CREATION PROCESS: SIX STEPS

Co-creation is a process of listening intently to your customer while working together to co-design consumer solutions that currently do not exist.

This process occurs during face-to-face or online community discussions, but can also occur with an intermediary—such as a retailer—who sells to and influences the sale of a product to a consumer.

The six-step co-creation model can be used with a consumer or any other influencer of a sale. The following example would be for any

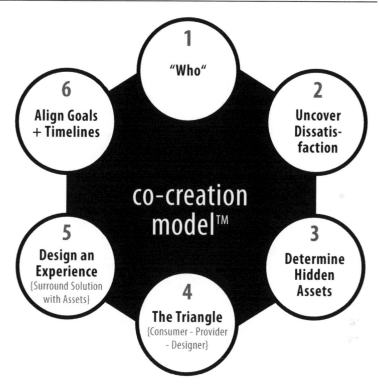

company that sells products, services, or ideas through a retailer, distributor, or any other business.

STEP 1: WHO SHOULD BE PART OF CO-CREATION MEETING?

Depending on product nuances and customer needs, the optimal co-creation discussion requires the participation of marketers, designers, packaging, and sales leadership. The best co-creation meetings also include a third-party facilitator who helps the consumer and the retailer share the trends that are on their mind while the designers and marketers sit back and listen. Like any team or meeting, the optimal number of people depends on the chemistry of the people and the complexity of the solution.

STEP 2: UNCOVER DISSATISFACTION

During the initial discovery step, the executive team must take the time to conduct a rich diagnosis of the customer's unmet needs, emerging trends, hunches, and societal shifts. In the consumer packaged goods industry, it's vital that the manufacturer understand the retailer or distributor's corporate priorities, competitive threats, and areas of potential new business.

During this phase, it is necessary to understand why these themes are important to customers, and to provide deeper clarity into motives, aspirations, and corporate needs. The deeper you understand the consumer's agenda, the more relevant you will become in their eyes. The more relevant you become in their eyes, the higher probability that you together can create a better experience or product for the end-user you are both trying to please.

STEP 3: DETERMINE HIDDEN ASSETS

Prior to sitting down with the retail customer or the consumer, take the time to assess your corporate hidden assets—tangible and intangible. Your most valuable and relevant assets will be those that address your customer's largest dissatisfactions while creating a compelling experience and stronger brand loyalty. Here are some examples of assets that are many times underutilized and undervalued:

- » UNIQUE BRANDS OR TECHNOLOGIES HOUSED IN OTHER DIVISIONS OF A COMPANY
- » EMERGING INSIGHTS AND A DEEP KNOWLEDGE OF THE SHOPPER AND CONSUMER
- » AN AGILE CULTURE THAT UTILIZES CUSTOMIZATION TO PERSONALIZE A PRODUCT OR SERVICE
- » CORE CUSTOMER DATABASES REFLECTING WHY THEIR CONSUMERS ARE NOT LOYAL
- » DOMESTIC AND INTERNATIONAL CONSUMER AND SHOPPER MEGATRENDS RIGHT AROUND THE CORNER
- » KNOWLEDGE INTO EMERGING SOCIETAL TRENDS THAT ARE INFLUENCING THE CONSUMER
- » UNIQUE THIRD-PARTY STRATEGIC ALLIANCES WITH INDUSTRY INFLUENCERS THAT CAN HELP CREATE AN EVEN DEEPER AND STRONGER CONSUMER EXPERIENCE

STEP 4: THE TRIANGLE: CONSUMER/PROVIDER/DESIGNER

Over the years, many retail merchandising executives have shared with me their frustration over not being involved in the product design process. They historically have been involved in the discussions, but only as a formality. What a wasted opportunity for strengthening the overall solution! Often these intermediaries offer a unique competitive vantage point to the designer or manufacturer of a product. These influencers have a very precise and broad impression of the consumer's needs and trends surrounding them.

During co-creation meetings, the retailer or distributor is asked to share their creative ideas, business goals, and insights into unmet consumer needs. The manufacturer or marketer then shares those insights from the consumer's perspective and discusses ways to improve the product. Since most organizations have a very difficult time remaining objective, a skilled industry facilitator who understands both parties' interests can help foster alignment.

STEP 5: DESIGN AN EXPERIENCE

Prior to sitting down with your customer for a co-creation discussion, review their boardroom priorities, areas of dissatisfaction, your assets, and their corporate goals. Most companies initially start their customer engagements focusing on their own goals versus the goals of their customers. The closer your goals align with your customers' personal and financial priorities, the higher the probability of creating a product that delivers a real impact for everyone.

STEP 6: ALIGN GOALS AND TIMELINES

After reviewing all comments, suggestions, and ideas, it is necessary that a time of reflection be agreed upon to summarize and synthesize those feedback. An important practice is to agree on the most relevant next steps, project goals, and sensible timelines, and to set a follow-up meeting.

One of the best practices in co-creation is to agree upfront that the role of the meeting is to scan and evaluate the landscape looking for valuable ideas. Another benefit is that further evaluation and deeper reflection will occur after the meeting, allowing for objectivity in the innovation process. In other words, it is always good business to state that all parties need to *reflect* on the ideas that surfaced prior to taking further action.

The best companies at co-creation are agile and fast-moving, but they also reserve the right to say no to an idea they are not comfortable moving forward on. A disciplined methodology allows the team to unpack new ideas while sensibly driving results.

CO-CREATION ROLE MODELS

Dark horse leaders are not buried in self-observation or self-obsession. When they are in front of their customers, they "give undivided presence to the present," to quote Hollywood director John Frankenheimer. They don't believe in muting the voices of critics, and they are not ashamed of offering up the wrong answer. They look at the creative process as one of uncovering what's already there, versus carrying the burden of creating something anew. Wherever they find an innovation is fine with them!

The following are just a few examples of the most effective companies at utilizing co-creation strategy.

DENTEK
UNIQUE PRODUCTS AT FAST-FOOD SPEED

If you talk with smaller oral care companies about DenTek Oral Care, you will hear a couple of common themes. First, how the heck do they knock off other people's ideas so quickly, make it better, and sell it cheaper? Second, they must have a great relationship with the top retailers because they seem to have a constant stream of products (every six months) that magically appears on the store shelves.

Having personally led the sales development team at DenTek, I observed up close how this company maximized the innovation process through co-creation discovery meetings. Every new item was informally presented to Wal-Mart, Target, CVS, and Walgreens up to a year before the initial new item presentation. This precaution is a co-creation step that uncovers roadblocks and determines the retailer's level of interest *prior to ever making a capital investment or making a product.* Here I learned that, good news or bad, constructive criticism could only strengthen us; we did not move a muscle until we had acted on the feedback of our retailers, tailoring our products to satisfy their specific needs.

The idea of sitting down and discussing a potential new item before everything is buttoned up is a challenge most companies are not willing to embrace. Dark horses cannot be afraid of the unknown, unfinished, or imperfect—such ideas can be perfected in the co-creation process. Many companies might consider this collaborative approach a bit edgy, but DenTek lives and thrives on that edge.

DenTek brought a passion for creating unique oral care devices with the speed of a fast-food restaurant. Every six months, DenTek sat down with their top retail partners to review product ideas, often customizing products for that retailer based on their unique requirements. This is why, historically, DenTek would produce different configurations or unique sizes of a product in one retailer and not in another. They were the masters of *selling what the customer wants, not what they wanted to sell.*

Lex Shankle, who led DenTek's marketing for ten years and was pivotal in helping the company double in size, lays out the steps they would take in the co-creation process:

1. OVERLAY AND INTERPRET THE CONSUMER DATA WITH THE SYNDICATED DATA LOOKING FOR IDEAS.
2. ASK THE SHOPPERS WHY THEY LIKE BUYING OUR PRODUCTS.
3. SPEAK WITH THE RETAILERS ABOUT THEIR UNMET PRODUCT NEEDS.
4. QUICKLY COLLABORATE WITH THE RETAILERS TO HELP CO-DESIGN THE NEXT GROUP OF INNOVATIONS. [4]

That's co-creation on multiple levels!

DenTek won't move an inch unless they run their innovation ideas by their top retailer partners.

YES TO INC.
TREATED AS PART OF WALGREENS' TEAM

The Yes To Inc. brand gained a strong foothold in the market by picking Walgreens as their first key strategic partner to create and launch their most innovative new products. The Walgreens consumer is perfectly aligned with the Yes To brand, and they also serve the role of brand advocate and influencer.

"We chose Walgreens as our primary partner to introduce the brand, but during the negotiations we realized that Walgreens also *chose us*," says Yes To co-founder Ido Leffler. "We were in sixteen stores first, and they wanted to provide this for their customer. They embraced our mission, vision, and values and truly partnered with us and appreciated our tenacity. Initially we had limited manufacturing and emotional capacity, but Walgreens treated us like we were part of their team. As the brand started to take off, Walgreens became a great proof statement for our company."

Leffler says he believes that business is not done through email; it is done by breaking bread and sharing experiences. In his words, "Winning business is accomplished through relationships. I want to see you first, and then get to know you personally. Then I will share my business plan… You make people feel welcome in your home and in your business. This product innovation philosophy was pivotal in the co-creation process with Walgreens." [5]

APOLLO HEALTH AND BEAUTY CARE
EXCEEDING CLIENT EXPECTATIONS

Apollo Health and Beauty Care—one of the fastest growing private brand companies in their sector—collaborates with only the best marketing agencies, formulators, package designers, and trend researchers.

As co-founder Charles Wachsberg shared, "Our partners are like family, we are that intertwined in each other's business. That is the reason that we hire very slowly and evaluate potential partners and associates through a long dynamic interview process. On the flip side, if we notice that we have made a cultural mistake with a hire, we move very swiftly. Our partners and associates must love to create, have a passion for excellence, love the details, customer development, and must love to serve."

When your business model is creating custom brands and designs for many diverse and multifaceted retailers across North America and beyond, you must have a keen awareness of cultural trends and emerging consumer shifts. Wachsberg passionately lays out his company's mandate that they will

» BE GLOBALLY RELEVANT,
» INVEST IN FUTURE TRENDS, AND
» MAINTAIN A SPEED-TO-MARKET MODEL THAT IS ALWAYS BEST IN ITS PEER CLASS AND WHICH CAN DELIVER A NEW AND CUSTOMIZED PRODUCT PORTFOLIO FROM SCRATCH IN LESS THAN FOUR MONTHS.

Wachsberg says, "We are not married to an idea, a product form, or a current delivery system. We are instead passionately committed to delighting and exceeding the expectations of our clients."

A good example of Apollo's co-creation culture occurred after GOJO Industries sold PURELL to Pfizer Consumer Healthcare. Within twenty-four months of the acquisition of PURELL, Apollo collaborated with several food, mass, and drug retailers on the design of uniquely

Chicago's own Sunset Foods—where buying groceries is a service event!

positioned and sensory leading hand sanitizers. Apollo created a custom set of products with diverse formulas, fragrances, and delivery systems including sprays and foams. Apollo lives for creating products that fill voids in consumer and retailers' minds through co-creation.[6]

SUNSET FOODS
CO-CREATION IN AISLE 1

If you ever find yourself on the north side of Chicago, I encourage you to visit one of a handful of smaller independent grocery stores called Sunset Foods. These stores are embedded in a number of affluent Chicago communities and are surrounded by—and competing with— many of the largest national food chains in America: Wal-Mart, Target, Trader Joe's, Costco, and Jewel-Osco, which is owned by Albertsons. These major food operators control more than 60 percent of the groceries sold in the Chicago area and have a lock on the market. But no one ever told Sunset Foods!

This visionary, privately held grocery group has called Chicago home since 1937, and the owners clearly place a premium on giving back to the communities they serve. Sunset Foods supports nearly three hundred local organizations each year by participating in fundraising activities, sponsoring a variety of events, and making monetary donations.

Sunset Foods has transformed buying groceries into a service event. The flavor of the experience was co-created with their valued customers.

» IN STORE, YOU ARE SURROUNDED BY UNIQUE SPECIALTY, GOURMET, HEALTH, AND ORGANIC FOODS REMINISCENT OF A EUROPEAN BAKERY.

» AN INTEGRATED ONLINE AND IN-STORE CUSTOMER SERVICE SPECIALIST IS ON HAND TO HELP YOU WITH YOUR CATERING, PARTY, BIRTHDAY, PICNIC, AND CORPORATE MEETING NEEDS.

» THERE ARE MORE IN-STORE SERVICE SPECIALISTS PER CUSTOMER THAN THE LARGER CHAINS THEY COMPETE AGAINST THROUGHOUT CHICAGO. THEY HELP YOU TO YOUR CAR, COORDINATE CATERING, CARRY A LARGE ORDER TO THE CASH REGISTER, OR RUN TO A SHELF TO PICK UP AN ITEM YOU MAY HAVE FORGOTTEN.

» ANGUS AND PRIME MEATS, WINES, CHEESES, AND DELI NEEDS ARE WRAPPED INTO A STORE THAT IS A THIRD THE SIZE OF ITS COMPETITORS.

» THEY CARRY A UNIQUE ARRAY OF NATURAL AND ORGANIC HEALTH AND BEAUTY CARE PRODUCTS NORMALLY RESERVED FOR RETAILERS SUCH AS WHOLE FOODS OR VITAMIN STORES.

» PROMPT GROCER HOME DELIVERY IS PROVIDED WITH ACCURACY, CONSISTENCY, AND WITH A GENEROUS SMILE ON THE FACE OF THE HOME DELIVERY PERSON.[7]

SUNSET FOODS

Stock your empty fridge and save $**10** OFF
your first grocery purchase at Sunset Foods!

Welcome new neighbor! As you settle into your new home, Sunset Foods invites you to surround yourself in comfort – food, that is. Stop by and pick up the foods you love, and save $10 on your first in-store purchase with this postcard.*

Experience the Sunset Foods difference:
• Gourmet grocer without gourmet prices
• Family-owned and operated for 75 years with five convenient locations
• Superior customer service – we unload your cart, we bag your groceries and load your car too!
• Unique in-store events – from wine tastings and celebrity chef demos, to complimentary cooking and nutrition classes

And much more! Stop by your neighborhood Sunset Foods today and discover why we've been named Chicagoland's favorite grocery store.

*One-time use only. Postcard must be presented at time of purchase. Present Sunset Associate Enter PLU at checkout in aisles # 0. Discount. PLU #16 *$40 purchase required (liquor and cigarettes excluded).

BONUS GIFT: Introduce yourself to our store manager and receive a FREE reusable shopping bag.

High-quality artisan breads, farmstead cheeses, local offerings, and fresh fish flown in daily are the essence of why new patrons join the Sunset Foods experience

One Sunset Foods customer said to me, "It is almost like they are waiting for me to ask for something they don't have, so they can go out and find it for me." She went on, "There are products in this store I can't find anywhere else, anywhere. And if they don't have it on the shelf, they will go find it for me. There is nothing like Sunset Foods." They are one of the best at co-creating a distinct grocery assortment offering tailored to the individual needs of each consumer living in the neighborhood.

This little organization lives for customer service. All members of the Sunset Foods team walk around the store waiting for questions; they make recommendations and scope out any unmet customer needs. They are looking for co-creation right in the middle of the aisle!

Are you hardwired to your customers' needs? Do you understand their deepest areas of dissatisfaction? The new economy provides an opportunity for organizations to create customized products or services, and co-developed by their most loyal customers.

Where are you in the process?

INSIGHTS ON CO-CREATION

» CO-CREATION IS A CATALYST FOR IMPROVING THE INNOVATION PROCESS.

» CO-CREATION IS AN OPEN CULTURE THAT EMPHASIZES LISTENING, GENERATING IDEAS WITH CUSTOMERS, AND EVALUATING IDEAS THAT MAY BE BUBBLING UP ON THE FRINGES OF YOUR INDUSTRY.

» CUSTOMERS CAN BOTH VALIDATE IDEAS AND SERVE AS A SOURCE FOR THEM, AND ARE LOYAL TO SOLUTIONS THEY CREATE.

» COMPANIES USING CO-CREATION EARN THE ROLE OF TRUSTED ADVISORS WITH THEIR CUSTOMERS.

» EFFECTIVE CO-CREATION INVOLVES UNCOVERING CUSTOMERS' UNSTATED NEEDS, EMERGING TRENDS, HUNCHES, SOCIETAL SHIFTS, COMPETITIVE LESSONS, AND SO ON.

» COMPANIES THAT POSSESS A MUCH DEEPER UNDERSTANDING OF THEIR CUSTOMERS' NEEDS CREATE STRONGER LOYALTY AND ADVOCACY WITH THESE CUSTOMERS BY PARTNERING WITH THEM THROUGH THE CO-CREATION INNOVATION PROCESS.

» DARK HORSE COMPANIES ARE ADEPT AT CREATING THE NEXT GENERATION OF INNOVATION; THEY UNDERSTAND CULTURAL INSIGHTS THAT DO NOT ALWAYS SHOW UP IN RESEARCH STUDIES. THEY ARE NOT BURIED IN SELF-OBSERVATION, RESEARCH, OR SELF-OBSESSION.

THOUGHT STARTERS

1. WHAT CAN YOU BRING TO A CUSTOMER RELATIONSHIP THAT CAN *CHANGE THE GAME?*

2. WHO ARE THE BEST IDEA PEOPLE IN YOUR ORGANIZATION, AND HOW DO YOU FREE THEM UP TO CREATE?

3. HOW CAN YOU CREATE A DEEPER *CONSUMER EXPERIENCE* THAT APPEALS TO YOUR CORE CUSTOMERS' UNMET NEEDS AND PERSONAL EMOTIONS?

4. SINCE IT IS NEVER JUST ABOUT SIZE, WHAT ARE YOUR MOST DIFFERENTIATING IDEAS OR INTANGIBLES THAT POSITION YOU AS IRREPLACEABLE?

5. WHICH OF YOUR TOP CUSTOMERS SHOULD YOU MEET WITH QUARTERLY TO BETTER UNDERSTAND THEIR NEXT GENERATION OF NEEDS?

6. WHAT COMPETITORS SEEM TO BEAT YOU TO THE IDEA BANK, AND HOW CAN YOU OUTPERFORM THEM IN THIS AREA?

7. HOW DO YOU BUILD UNIQUE KNOWLEDGE IN YOUR ORGANIZATION, AND IS THIS KNOWLEDGE BEING PASSED ON DOWN THE LINE?

8. HOW CAN YOU MORE EFFECTIVELY UNDERSTAND THE EMERGING AND FUTURE NEEDS OF YOUR CUSTOMERS, AND HOW CAN YOU *OWN* THAT EMERGING NEED?

Chapter 6:

THE

BLUEPRINT

STRATEGY IS EXECUTION

It is well known that "problem avoidance" is an important part of problem solving... You go upstream and alter the system so that the problem does not occur in the first place.

—EDWARD DE BONO, CREATIVITY EXPERT

The vast majority of product launches, reorganizations, mergers, and improvement initiatives either fail or grossly disappoint. In all, roughly 90 percent of major projects violate their own schedule, budget, or quality standards.[1]

Obviously, these performance gaps are not part of the plan. Companies that work together to create very concise business plans, supported by a constant rhythm of team meetings, are more apt to stay on course and execute their plans with precision.

It seems obvious, so why do most initiatives break down? Let me make it very clear. The challenges are twofold: lack of alignment around the company's priorities, and lack of trust in talking honestly with leadership. When employees don't commit to (or don't understand) the plan, or are afraid of bringing forward bad news, you get results like:

» 95 PERCENT OF EMPLOYEES ARE UNABLE TO DEFINE THEIR CORPORATE STRATEGY.[2]
» 88 PERCENT OF EMPLOYEES SURVEYED WERE CURRENTLY WORKING ON PROJECTS OR INITIATIVES THEY PREDICTED WOULD EVENTUALLY FAIL—AND YET THEY CONTINUED TO PLOD ALONG. MOST AGREED THAT A "SLOW-MOTION TRAIN WRECK" WAS THE EXPRESSION THAT BEST DESCRIBED THE STATE OF THEIR CURRENT PROJECT.
» FEWER THAN 10 PERCENT OF RESPONDENTS SAID IT WAS DEEMED ACCEPTABLE TO SPEAK OPENLY AT WORK ABOUT WHAT WAS GOING WRONG.[3]

Organizations that openly create their business blueprint and honestly discuss their progress and failures are in a better position to get the best out of their team while achieving their goals.

So what is in an effective strategic blueprint? In my years of working with companies big and small, I've noted the techniques that work, and techniques that don't. I've adopted those most effective approaches in my own practice, and strongly advise my clients do the same. Your company, too, should clearly define your strategic blueprint, a simple outline of your team's positioning and business plan. Topics can include:

» ANNUAL PRIORITIES
» KEY DRIVERS AND HIDDEN ASSETS
» INSIGHTS INTO THE CUSTOMER AND THE COMPETITION
» DESCRIPTION OF THE COMPANY'S IDENTITY AND PURPOSE
» AN EXPLANATION OF WHY YOU ARE DIFFERENT
» INDIVIDUAL PERSONAL GOALS
» RISK ASSESSMENTS
» RESOURCE NEEDS AND SCENARIO PLANS
» DEFINITION OF ANNUAL AND LONGER TERM GOALS
» SUMMARY OF GAME CHANGING IDEAS

A good blueprint answers the following questions:

» **WHAT** IS THE TEAM'S PURPOSE; WHAT'S THE CONTEXT WITHIN THE INDUSTRY, AND WHAT MUST BE DONE TO ACHIEVE COMPETITIVE AND FINANCIAL ADVANTAGE?
» **HOW** WILL THE ORGANIZATION ACHIEVE THE CORE OBJECTIVES, AND WHAT ARE THE RISKS TO ACHIEVING THE STATED GOALS?
» **WHO** IS THE CUSTOMER, AND WHO WITHIN THE ORGANIZATION IS RESPONSIBLE FOR LEADING THE KEY STRATEGIES AND DRIVING THE OBJECTIVES?
» **WHERE** MUST THE ORGANIZATION FOCUS TO ACHIEVE ADVANTAGES, AND WHAT ARE THE FUTURE NEEDS TO SUSTAIN AN ADVANTAGE?
» **WHEN** MUST THE ORGANIZATION ACHIEVE THE STATED ANNUAL OR LONGER TERM GOALS, AND WHEN DO INDIVIDUAL GOALS NEED TO BE ACHIEVED?

Companies that simplify these key questions and introduce them consistently into everyone's daily lives will drive stronger execution against whatever they are focusing on.

The challenge within most companies is the difficulty of blending strategy (or strategic thinking) and execution on a daily basis. Strategic discussions are not something done once or twice per year in an off-site meeting room; strategic reflection goes on *all the time* at dark horse companies. They pride themselves on always thinking strategically while holding themselves deeply accountable to daily execution. When

THE STRATEGIC BLUEPRINT

CONTEXT	DIAGNOSIS	SOLUTION	EXECUTION
Identity / Purpose	Influencers	Unique Sales Proposition	Eliminate Barriers
Societal Shifts	Customer Drivers	Annual Goals	Customer Plan
Hidden Assets	Vulnerabilities	Define Solution	Time Table
Business Risks	Penetration Plan	Package Solution	Communication Plan
Industry Context	Resource Needs	Marketing Programs	Individual Plans
Competition			Scorecard

advising executives on business strategy, I've seen the positive results of a company honestly addressing its identity, corporate roadblocks, hidden assets, and alignment challenges.

Companies should think of their blueprint as a living, breathing document: one to be discussed, debated, and refined. They need to be able to think critically and adjust their strategy when necessary. In other words, hold your values and modify your strategy. How well do you think *your* company understands the competitive landscape, business strategies, industry alignment, and your customers' most important priorities?

Let's see how you do with these strategic blueprint questions.

ARE YOU MAXIMIZING SALES GROWTH?

1. WHAT ARE THE THREE COMPANY ASSETS THAT TRULY DIFFERENTIATE YOU FROM THE REST, AND DO YOUR CUSTOMERS VALUE THESE ASSETS?

2. ARE YOU RELEVANT, AND ARE YOU THE ONLY ONES WHO DO WHAT YOU DO? HOW DO YOU KNOW?

3. DOES YOUR COMPANY POSITIONING DELIVER CONSISTENT RESULTS AND COMPETITIVE INSULATION?

4. DO YOU THINK YOUR OVERALL COST OF SALES IS WHERE IT SHOULD BE? WHAT'S YOUR BENCHMARK?

5. WHAT ARE YOUR TOP-FIVE CORPORATE PRIORITIES, AND IS EVERYONE COLLECTIVELY WORKING ON THEM?

6. HOW HAVE YOU CHOSEN YOUR TOP CUSTOMERS, AND ARE THEY RESOURCED APPROPRIATELY TO ACHIEVE THE NECESSARY OUTCOMES OUTLINED IN YOUR BLUEPRINT?

7. IS YOUR SALES ORGANIZATION CREATING NEW VALUE WHICH ALIGNS WITH THE TOP PRIORITIES OF YOUR TOP CUSTOMERS?

8. DO YOU HAVE THE RIGHT PEOPLE WITH THE RIGHT SKILLS IN YOUR SALES LEADERSHIP TEAM AND IS THAT YOUR NUMBER ONE BUSINESS OBJECTIVE?

9. DOES YOUR SALES COMPENSATION REWARD BUILDING CUSTOMER LOYALTY AND LONGER TERM SUCCESS?

10. ARE YOUR SALES AND MARKETING TEAMS ALIGNED AND HARDWIRED TO YOUR CUSTOMERS' AGENDA?

How did you do?

All organizations, even the best, struggle to stay aligned with the key components of their blueprint. Creating a disciplined sales strategy supported by the rhythm of ongoing team meetings and reflection helps organizations stay close to their plan.

So then, why do many of us fight the process of creating this type of blueprint?

There may be a lack of planning discipline and administration skills, or there may be a fear of looking in the mirror and seeing cracks in the operation. But whether you look in the mirror or not, the cracks remain. Dark horse companies are not afraid of modifying their plans in response to changing dynamics around them. They are good at wrestling with the brutal facts, allowing them a competitive advantage. Businesses could learn quite a bit by modeling the creative approach of artists.

I'm reminded of the words of one musical artist in particular. In preparation for the launch of U2's *How to Dismantle an Atomic Bomb*, the band's singer, Bono, shared his approach to music creation: "After creating a new song we do everything but take its head off, and then we try to rebuild it. If the song stands, it is worth putting on the record." [4]

I've found that there's a valuable lesson in that level of honesty and openness that allows an artist to birth a song and then disruptively tear it apart to see if it stands. The lesson is that the best business executives are artists; they create value, transfer emotion, and create consumer experiences. Great company blueprints, like songs, must *be open to being wrong.*

Many of the dark horse companies we have evaluated are courageous about cutting their losses when they are wrong. When you have introduced a failing proposition, you know it very quickly. Dark horse companies do not keep dying products or services on life support; they carefully, yet decisively, pull the plug.

This is not the case for many companies, because once you design and launch a plan, the tendency is to defend or justify the poor

Artists understand that innovation must stand up under immense pressure. The best artists constantly reinvent themselves a number of times through the candid assessment of their craft.

performance. I understand the struggle; revising your plans is hard work that demands transparency and vulnerability.

Many of the dark horse companies we have studied are fanatical about the discipline of creating a clear sales blueprint. More than that, they commit to the culture of ongoing open discussion around modifying and improving their blueprint. It is an ongoing process; it's fluid, and everyone is invited to contribute to the plan.

So then, is there a need for the annual strategic-planning meeting?

Yes, dark horse companies conduct annual planning meetings to evaluate what they want to become three to five years out. Many of the companies outlined in this book work under a very flexible culture, freeing them to go after opportunities in the moment. But they also set aside time several times a year to discuss vision, competitive conditions, customer engagements, innovation, and training. It is not a process, but part of their daily dialogue.

THE UMBRELLA SALES POSITION

Each of us is a brand and we stand for something in the eyes of our friends, employers, and customers. What do you stand for and why are you different? The best brands, big or small, have personality and are distinct. They stand for something special, are difficult to copy, are authentic, and they understand what their audience needs.

The most successful dark horse companies are also great storytellers, and are adept at sharing their story with their customers. Within their story is a crisp line or two that describes why the company and their services are *special and irreplaceable*. This is their positioning, or what I refer to as their umbrella sales position.

An umbrella sales position is a simplified elevator pitch (i.e., a one-minute speech) that explains your value. Companies that are skilled at this have figured out why they are different, and they understand how to create an experience that is more than the base product they are selling. Remember Grateful Dead frontman Jerry Garcia's idea? "You don't want to be the best of the best. You just want to be the only one who does what you do."

I firmly believe that a unique umbrella position creates a meaningful buffer between you and any competitor. This position is often at the axis

Your Distinct Team Identity

COMPETITOR

YOU

A COMPELLING UMBRELLA POSITION

A clear umbrella position differentiates you from competition.

COMPETITOR

COMPETITOR

Your Valuable Assets

of your company or team's identity and your most distinct and valuable tangible and intangible assets. This is the location on the competitive map where you have the *potential* to be the only one who does what you do.

I can't tell you the numbers of times I have heard underperforming companies say, "We don't have time for strategy," or "We do our own strategy and don't need assistance." The whole idea of *ongoing* strategy isn't comfortable to them.

Winners understand that strategy is execution. One fuels the other, and one is a catalyst for the other. Strategic thinking and tight execution must go hand in hand.

CHECKLISTS: VISIBILITY, THOUGHTFULNESS, DISCIPLINE

A few years back, Harvard surgeon and *New Yorker* staff writer Atul Gawande authored *The Checklist Manifesto*. His message is that the complexity of life has exceeded most individuals' ability to manage their lives consistently without error, despite advances in technology, training, and specialization. His solution is to use checklists to ensure success. Yet, despite demonstrating that checklists produce results, there is resistance to their use; checklists—or blueprints—demand *visibility, thoughtfulness,* and *discipline.*

Gawande believes that in a complex environment, we are all up against two challenges. First, we have lapses in memory; second, people skip simple steps within routines because the routines have become mundane. If the truth be known, we love the discipline of an organization when it serves us, but most of us would rather improvise because it demands less of us.

I've found that the top business performers are laser-focused against their most vital metrics, and they talk about them at every opportunity.

What should ideally be on your sales checklist?

In 2008 the World Health Organization (WHO) established a set of surgical safety guidelines or checklists to improve the safety of patients undergoing surgical procedures. The surgical checklist defined three distinct phases of an operation, each relating to a component in the procedure. These phases are the steps prior to inducing anesthesia, the steps before the incision, and then validating that the appropriate activities have occurred prior to the patient leaving the operating facility. In each phase, a checklist coordinator validates that the surgical team has completed the appropriate listed steps before proceeding to the next phase in the procedure.

Many dark horse companies review a disciplined set of metrics at each of their business meetings, similar to the surgeon before a big procedure. The culture encourages systemic evaluation of all parts of the business, facilitates transparency, and improves outcomes.

MEIJER
MASTERING MOMENTS OF SUDDEN IMPACT

I asked one of the top executives at the Grand Rapids, Michigan regional retailer Meijer Inc. why some companies succeed and others fail with their business plans. He shared five blind spots to an effective sales blueprint:

1. LEADERS DON'T UNDERSTAND WHICH VITAL RESOURCES ARE NEEDED TO BE SUCCESSFUL.
2. THE WHOLE TEAM IS NOT HELD ACCOUNTABLE TO MONTHLY, QUARTERLY, AND ANNUAL RESULTS. THIS LEVEL OF DETAIL DRIVES A COMPANY FORWARD AND EVERYONE STAYS HUNGRY.
3. CORPORATE COMPLACENCY DUE TO SUCCESS AND PREVIOUS ACCOMPLISHMENT.
4. POOR PREPARATION AND A LOW ATTENTION TO DETAIL.
5. A CULTURE THAT DOES NOT PROACTIVELY CHALLENGE THE FINANCIALS AND LOOK FOR NEW OPPORTUNITIES.

Meijer is a very detail-oriented corporate culture, and their blueprint for success guides their daily business management. Their blueprint is supported by clear core values and constant training and development; their level of preparation and diligence mirrors the leadership philosophy of historic Michigan Wolverines coach Bo Schembechler. Under Schembechler, the Michigan program taught a principle known as "sudden change"—legendary in Michigan football lore. Sudden-change cultures have mastered the ability to take a moment of crisis and turn it into their finest moment of triumph. [5]

Meijer Inc. does not get surprised too often, and when they do, they try to turn challenge into advantage. It is part of their identity and is a philosophy driving their success blueprint.

Let's revisit three other companies that differentiate themselves through their disciplined strategic blueprint.

WAHL HOME PRODUCTS
TRUE NORTH

Wahl Home Products utilizes their own blueprint, which Bruce Kramer, VP of Sales and Marketing, describes as "True North—that means maximizing global profit and sales and stretching with integrity." The True North idea was birthed by Wahl president, Greg Wahl, and is the lifeblood of their corporate culture. "We balance strategic thinking and strategic planning, meeting twice per year, setting the blueprint, and reviewing the plan all throughout the year," says Kramer. This is very different from their strategic planning process, which encompasses a week of thinking and summarizing the goals and values of the company's five-year plan. One encompasses vision and values and the other is strategic thinking married with execution planning.

The Wahl consumer blueprint is comprised of six themes that drive the organization:

> » CREATING PRODUCTS THAT TRULY ADDRESS UNMET CONSUMER NEEDS.
> » CREATING NEW PRODUCTS FOUNDED ON RESEARCH AND LED BY INSIGHTS.
> » INCORPORATING DESIGN AND CRAFTSMANSHIP INTO ALL PRODUCTS AND MARKETING.
> » LOOKING TO IMPROVE THE CURRENT PRODUCT LINE THROUGH ADDITIONAL ATTRIBUTES OR ADDED VALUE BENEFITS.
> » SPEAKING TO THE CONSUMER, CLEARLY AND LOUDLY, ABOUT ALL NEW PRODUCT INTRODUCTIONS.
> » BALANCING A MULTICHANNEL SALES STRATEGY THAT EFFECTIVELY DISTRIBUTES BRANDS THROUGH DRUGSTORES, MASS-MARKET, DEPARTMENT, AND SPECIALTY STORES.

Everything about Wahl's sales and marketing blueprint screams intimacy, design, and love of product. As Kramer puts it, "Others go out and have someone make their products, but Wahl creates them."[6]

BEIERSDORF
DISCIPLINE AND PROCESS CAN SET YOU FREE

We live in a world where speed and agility are the currency of the new economy. Whoever launches their product first often has an advantage. Sports teams who move quickly to attract free agents can move from the middle of the pack to the front as the favorites within their division. Politicians who act decisively are often given kudos for perceived courage and leadership. It is no wonder that aggressiveness is often rewarded more than thoughtful discipline.

The Beiersdorf USA culture is a paradox at first glance. The organization grounds itself in details, driving, advocating, and listening. They engage customers on the importance of excellence in execution, while striving to create a blueprint that focuses big ideas. According to Beiersdorf North America President and General Manager Bill Graham, "We are a smaller, unique organization, and winning requires that we think big, while looking and playing different than P&G and Unilever."

Beiersdorf's global focus is skin care, and they have a vision of achieving either a number one or number two market position within every segment they play in. While most organizations focus on where to expand their business, Beiersdorf focuses equally as much on where not to play, providing clarity of purpose and stronger execution. This philosophy resulted in the divestiture of many non-skin care items, including the large Futuro line of therapy knee wraps, braces, and compression stocking products. During the same time, the company expanded into several new skin care related categories, including lip care and bath and body shower products, which resulted in nearly doubling the size of their skin care footprint in the United States.

Eliminating a profitable and growing brand might seem like a difficult and risky move for any organization, but within the context of a larger blueprint, the trade-off created stronger expertise in their core skin care business. Divesting these non-core brands has provided Beiersdorf with laser focus in their core skin care categories.

Beiersdorf is an aggressive company that believes "people move companies," while discipline and process can set organizations free to innovate. Beiersdorf tries to walk the radical middle of a high attention

Beiersdorf's philosophy and blueprint brings a high attention to detail grounded in big ideas. Recently Nivea served as a sponsor of New Year's Rockin' Eve in New York City, creating great visibility and retail participation.

to detail with every part of their business. They believe in the power of a disciplined blueprint, but will never lose the power of being nimble in making business decisions. [7]

RICOLA
PROTECT EMPLOYEES

"A large portion of our business blueprint is protecting our employees," says Ricola president Bill Higgins.

"If you protect your team, they will protect the customers. Our team will take risks to protect our customers—even if the customers' requests are different than their needs. Another component of the Ricola business roadmap is ensuring that our brand and culture remain trusted at all costs. Ricola was natural before natural products were cool or even on the radar screen. The origins of the brand were based on a quirky yet creditable and trustworthy image."

Higgins recalls the Ricola advertisement highlighting the older Swiss man blowing the alpenhorn. "It was so bad it was great. That home-grown advertising campaign grew the brand organically for years. It was not corporate, and our most trusted consumers trusted us, and they still do."

Ricola's Higgins reminded me that you need a true balance of strategy and execution. It is not a 50/50 ratio, but it is pretty close, he says. On one trip to Switzerland to visit his corporate office, Higgins went mountain climbing and learned an important lesson about the Swiss leadership. "Walking in the mountains with ropes around you (connected literally and figuratively) is a real metaphor for the company and our culture," he notes. "You learn that at times you must jump over a crevasse, but often times walking slowly and patiently is imperative; that is the Ricola blueprint for success.[8]

Strategy and execution operate as one in dark horse companies. The most effective strategy is:

> » INTEGRATED INTO THE CULTURE
> » PRACTICAL IN NATURE
> » EXECUTABLE IN ONE'S DAILY OPERATIONS AND ALIGNED TO CORE VALUES

There are many ways of constructing a business blueprint, but the best include an accurate assessment of *who* they are, *why* they are special, *where* they are going, *how* they will win, and *when* they will win.

An effective blueprint concisely outlines a company's reason for being, distinct competitive advantages, core consumer segment, future innovation plans, and their business model, and assesses risk and competitive vulnerabilities.

Most importantly, a successful blueprint must be streamlined enough to be discussed throughout the year in team planning meetings. The blueprint system is not a corporate event; it is a way of thinking. And the best organizations make it an integral part of their culture. The following themes are methodically addressed as part of the company rhythm:

- » A COMPANY'S IDENTITY
- » THEIR UMBRELLA POSITIONING (UNIQUE SALES PROPOSITION)
- » THE CONTEXT OF A BUSINESS
- » SOCIETAL SHIFTS AFFECTING BUSINESS
- » PROFIT MODEL (WHERE ARE YOU MAKING YOUR MONEY?)
- » BARRIERS TO GROWTH
- » MOST COMPELLING ASSETS THAT MATTER TO YOUR CUSTOMERS
- » COMPETITIVE THREATS
- » CORE STRATEGIES
- » INTENT AND BUSINESS PURPOSE
- » TALENT ASSESSMENT
- » TOP CUSTOMERS AND THEIR STATED NEEDS
- » LARGE CUSTOMER GOALS
- » RESOURCE NEEDS
- » INFLUENCER ACTION PLAN
- » A SUMMARY OF EACH INDIVIDUAL'S ANNUAL GOALS

We have seen, up close, that effective business blueprinting does make a difference. The most distinct dark horse companies live and breathe their strategic blueprint, and it is a part of their daily dialogue.

Their strategy informs, inspires, and drives their execution.

INSIGHTS ON BLUEPRINTS

» MOST PRODUCT LAUNCHES, REORGANIZATIONS, AND IMPROVEMENT INITIATIVES EITHER FAIL OR DISAPPOINT DUE TO VIOLATION OF SCHEDULE, BUDGET, AND/OR QUALITY.

» COMPANIES NEED CONSISTENT TEAM INTEGRATION MEETINGS OR REFLECTION POINTS WHICH FACILITATE STRONGER EXECUTION AND GROWTH.

» COMPANIES SHOULD THINK OF THEIR BLUEPRINT AS A LIVING, BREATHING DOCUMENT, ONE TO BE DISCUSSED, DEBATED, AND REFINED. THEY NEED TO BE ABLE TO THINK CRITICALLY AND RECALIBRATE THEIR STRATEGY WHEN NECESSARY.

» THE MOST SUCCESSFUL DARK HORSE COMPANIES ARE ALSO GREAT STORYTELLERS, AND ARE ADEPT AT SHARING THEIR STORY WITH THEIR CUSTOMERS.

» WINNERS UNDERSTAND THAT STRATEGY IS EXECUTION. ONE FUELS THE OTHER, AND ONE IS A CATALYST FOR THE OTHER. STRATEGIC THINKING AND TIGHT EXECUTION MUST GO HAND IN HAND.

» DARK HORSES BELIEVE THAT STRATEGY IS AN EVERYDAY PART OF CORPORATE LIFE. THEY ARE ALWAYS THINKING ABOUT IDEAS, TRENDS, AND COMPETITORS' POSITIONING.

» DARK HORSE COMPANIES HAVE AN UMBRELLA SALES POSITIONING THAT IS UNIQUE IN THE CUSTOMER'S MIND.

THOUGHT STARTERS

1. ARE YOU TRULY DIFFERENT, AND HOW DO YOU IMPROVE DIFFERENTIATION?

2. WHAT ARE A COUPLE OF "SUDDEN CHANGE" MOMENTS THAT COULD DISRUPT YOUR BUSINESS, AND HOW WOULD YOU HANDLE THEM?

3. IS THERE ONE THING YOU ARE KNOWN FOR, AND CAN YOU CONVEY IT IN ONE SIMPLE SENTENCE?

4. DO YOU HAVE A ONE-PAGE SUMMARY OF YOUR BUSINESS THAT GUIDES YOU AND ALLOWS YOU TO BALANCE FUTURE INNOVATION AND DAILY EXECUTION?

5. WHAT IS GETTING IN THE WAY OF YOUR THREE MOST IMPORTANT GOALS?

6. WHAT PORTION OF YOUR BUSINESS WOULD BENEFIT FROM A CHECKLIST?

7. HOW ARE YOU AT BLENDING BOTH STRATEGY AND EXECUTION?

8. ARE YOUR TOP CUSTOMER GOALS REFLECTED IN YOUR BUSINESS PLAN?

Chapter 7:

INFLUENCERS

How's Your
Community?

He who influences the thoughts of his
times, influences all the times that follow.
He has made his impress on eternity.

—FRIEDRICH NIETZSCHE, PHILOSOPHER

If the behavior you want someone to adopt is not rewarding to them,
or linked to a deeply held belief system, most people will be creative
in coming up with arguments against the change. People aren't about
to give up what gives them intense pleasure or what constitutes an
important window into their identity simply because of your attempt at
persuasion.
[1] However, we do listen to people we trust, or people we don't know
personally but to whom we are attracted by their authority. In the short
film *Influencers: How Trends & Creativity Become Contagious,* filmmak-
ers Davis Johnson and Paul Rojanathara frame the idea that new ideas
are created and popularized by societal influencers who bring them to
the mainstream, after which the ideas often spread virally.

Many of our culture's most innovative and persuasive influencers—
such as rapper Jay-Z, Facebook's Mark Zuckerberg, health expert Dr.
Oz, and Oprah Winfrey—have a different way of thinking and express-
ing themselves. When they embrace an idea and incorporate it into
their lives, others watch and imitate. They are *early adopters*, and they
relish the role of transmitting ideas to others.

Early adopters, or opinion leaders, represent 13.5 percent of the
population. They are smarter than average and tend to be open to new

ideas. But they are different from innovators because they are socially connected and respected. And here's the real influence key: the rest of the population will not adopt the new practices until opinion leaders do.[2]

So what are the top three things everyone should know about opinion leaders or influencers?

» THEY SET THE TONE FOR WHETHER AN IDEA IS ACCEPTED OR WHETHER THE IDEA DIES ON THE VINE.
» INFLUENCERS NORMALLY CAN'T BE BOUGHT; YOU WIN THEM BY CAPTURING THEIR HEART AND VISION.
» INFLUENCERS EMBRACE AUTHENTICITY (AND THEY CAN SMELL A RAT).

Prior to a cultural shift, the general public is often slow to incorporate an idea into their lives. Even if the mainstream is slower to latch onto a new idea, they benefit from the drafting effect created by influencers who blaze the new trail.

Think of the numerous times celebrities have convincingly shined a light on third-world poverty issues or individual social justice causes. Sean Penn's efforts in Iraq and Haiti, Bob Geldof's leadership with Live Aid and Live 8, Angelina Jolie's concentrated focus on refugee problems in the Sudan, Pakistan, and Sierra Leone, and Bill and Melinda Gates' financial and strategic commitment to extreme poverty and to advancing education: these are just a few examples of influencers driving change.

So what does it take to become and remain an Opinion Leader or an Influencer?

» YOU MUST BE VIEWED AS KNOWLEDGEABLE ABOUT THE ISSUE AT HAND, AND STAY CONNECTED TO YOUR AREA OF EXPERTISE, OFTEN THROUGH A VARIETY OF SOURCES.
» YOU MUST BE VIEWED AS TRUSTWORTHY AND AS HAVING OTHER PEOPLE'S BEST INTERESTS IN MIND, WHILE USING KNOWLEDGE TO HELP OTHERS, NEVER MANIPULATING OR HARMING.

If others believe that you're missing either of these two qualities, you won't be very influential.[3] The more you attract and enlist these types of influencers and advocates to your vision, the higher the likelihood of broadening awareness of your product or service.

Influence is about storytelling. We influence others by creating a shared reality or a shared moment. Some call it a transfer of emotion from one person to another; it is infectious, creates momentum, and moves people into action.

The great persuader is personal experience. With persistent problems, it's best to help people experience the world as you experience it. Personal experience is the mother of all cognitive map changers. When trying to encourage others to change their long-established views, we should fight our inclination to persuade them through the clever use of verbal gymnastics and debate tricks. Instead, opt for a field trip; nothing changes a mind like the cold, harsh world hitting you with actual real-life data. [4]

The mission is to transform customers into advocates and enforcers of your brand, while empowering them to share their personal brand experiences with others. You see this phenomenon with dark horse companies that are rich in identity, full of influence themselves, and who attract influencers.

Let's take a look at three special companies that have created a community of passionate believers that love their brand, and love telling others about it even more.

AMY'S KITCHEN
VEGGIES AREN'T BORING

In 1987, the husband-and-wife team of Rachel and Andy Berliner birthed the vision of their company and named it after their newborn

Amy's Kitchen organic food business uses limited advertising and operates with targeted sampling events and educational events at retailers such as Whole Foods, Safeway, and Kroger.

daughter. Amy's Kitchen is an organic and natural brand that now extends across a number of categories including pizza, veggie-burgers, soups, burritos, salsas, and breakfast entries. Their brand positioning is simple: everything is vegetarian, organic, and never boring. [5]

How does Amy's Kitchen compete with the largest food manufacturers in the world? Their competitive differentiation is that they create distinct organic foods and utilize an array of in-store sampling and educational events through retailers that cater to their consumers—such as Whole Foods, Kroger, and Safeway. They also use targeted brand education in select organic magazines and health food shows, and they network with influencers who help build up their brand image. For example, Amy's Kitchen gained great visibility by being recognized in Oprah's O magazine for one of their new product launches.

There is a reason Amy's has been courted by a number of larger food companies over the years: their brand stands for something very authentic, and their food is delicious. As a result, Amy's Kitchen has both grown at a planned rate and stayed true to their identity.

DERMA E
GOOD GLOBAL CITIZENS

A portfolio of natural skin care items marrying purity, elegance, and efficacy, derma e is another brand that has a slew of consumer advocates. The brand is positioned as cruelty-free, paraben-free, and eco-friendly, and has a passionate following in natural health and wellness stores.

The company designs pure products for their consumers and is committed to both local and global causes. They have formed the Paraguay Project to create awareness for and address the daily struggles of the people of Paraguay. The vision was born when Sondra Miles, the daughter of one of the company's vice presidents (and herself a member of the team), was deeply moved by her personal experiences working as a Peace Corps volunteer in Paraguay. Observing firsthand the lack of education and sustainable incomes, the destruction of natural resources, and lack of female empowerment inspired the company to be a part of the solution.

derma e is a purpose-driven organization, serving a community of believers who want skin health and a way to make a difference.

In creating the Paraguay Project, derma e is trying to respond to those needs and create awareness about the struggles of the Paraguayan people. derma e purchases spider web lace at a fair price from women's groups who regularly sell their crafts in the markets in Asunción, Paraguay. All of the proceeds from lace sales are donated back to two Paraguayan non-profit organizations devoted to the protection of the rights of children and the preservation of the environment.[6]

The derma e organization addresses larger global challenges with their outreach to Paraguay, while benefiting from the "halo effect" of doing good. A percentage of all derma e sales is given to the Paraguay Project, the Special Olympics, and other charities. The brand team is also very smart about where they place their product offering —that is, only in certain retailers that fit their consumer profile and merchandising philosophies.

derma e is another example of a dark horse company using selective retail partners as influencers. Retailers such as Whole Foods, Ulta Beauty, Wegmans, and other natural food stores provide expanded shelf space, sampling initiatives, and educational materials to help build the brand. They also *win with few*.

STONYFIELD ORGANIC YOGURT
CUSTOMERS HAVING A COW

The cornerstone of a strong business is to move zealots of your brand from loyalty to advocacy. Most organizations love to spout off how loyal their top consumers are to their brand, but if the truth be known, very few people are that loyal to many brands. Dark horse companies don't need to create loyalty programs because they have more than a brand community on their side—they have believers. And if we are learning anything about social media and the role of viral marketing, we know that the size of the brand community does not necessarily indicate passion or commitment.

Stonyfield Organic Yogurt was born in 1983 with a commitment to healthy food, healthy people, and a healthy planet. Stonyfield is the leading organic yogurt company in the U.S., and the company has been involved in a long list of environmental and educational initiatives, thereby extending their name and influence beyond a cup of yogurt.

The New Hampshire-based business helps to support hundreds of family farms and keep more than 200,000 agricultural acres free of pesticides and chemicals commonly used on nonorganic farms and known to contaminate soil, drinking water, air, and food.[7]

Stonyfield uses a variety of social media and online tools to connect with consumers. The company's website has a detailed accounting of the ingredients in the products and how they are sourced. For the environmentally minded, the company's blog contains analyses of Stonyfield's environmental impact. Chairman Gary Hirshberg, a number of Stonyfield employees, and health and nutrition influencers blog, as do a few organic farmers. Consumers can even watch videos from some of the family farms that supply milk and other ingredients for Stonyfield's products.

Stonyfield's success is based on the passionate loyalty of its customers. It is, quite simply, what keeps the company running. Hirshberg tells how he was once approached by a customer in the dairy aisle in a Florida grocery store. She didn't recognize him—she wanted to tell him not to buy that other yogurt brand. She encouraged him to choose Stonyfield since it's made with whole foods, organic fruit, and no strange shelf stabilizers. Sadly, he didn't hire her to head up his consumer engagement team, but he did send her a much-deserved pack of coupons.[8]

How is *your* brand at creating community, advocacy, and emotional connection?

Stonyfield Organic Yogurt stays true to its beginnings of healthy food, people and a healthy planet.

WE ARE ALL BRANDS NOW

You are the message and your own style now counts as content. Whether you like it or not, we are all brands. Marc Gobé introduces this idea in *Emotional Branding*, where he articulates the necessity of positioning ourselves as not just brands, but as emotional brands. And the best, most compelling organizations embrace their identity as revivalists.

According to Gobé, emotional brands don't market to consumers or sell products; rather, they create deep authentic experiences that attract and fulfill personal desires. Emotional brands are aspirational and loved. They have character and charisma. The best emotional brands are not just seen, but *felt deeply.* [9]

In other words; it's all about gaining share of mind, share of emotion, share of imagination, and share of dreams. Breakthrough business relationships have very little to do with either the product or the service one represents; they are really about the value-added intangibles that accompany the product.

Business leaders can learn much from societal catalysts and zealots who operate in an atmosphere of revival. Enter Father Michael Pfleger...

FATHER MICHAEL PFLEGER
PEACE THROUGH DISRUPTION

What can a Catholic priest teach corporate America about transformational sales?

Father Michael Pfleger is that outspoken priest, and he's been at the center of many social justice debates in Chicago for the last twenty-five years. He is a transformational leader and an agent of social change. Picture a sixty-four-year-old white German Roman Catholic priest ministering on the Southside of Chicago in an African-American community, conducting 3½ hour church services that look like a Catholic mass led by a Southern preacher with a radical hint of Pentecostalism.

Father Mike is a walking paradox: a man of peace and a man of disruption. A somewhat polarizing figure, this man had challenged the leadership of the Catholic Church on numerous topics including racial reconciliation, the role of women in the ministry, the role of the church in society, and in areas of ecumenicalism. Father Mike is loved by most Protestant inner city church leaders (most of them African American and Latino), and is held at a distance by some of his priest peers.

He's well-known as the man who challenged Jerry Springer to clean up his act and reduce violence on his nationally syndicated television show—and won. Father Mike waged a nonviolent war against Springer through picketing, boycotts, and stand-ins.

He has orchestrated alternative nontraditional events facilitating peace within gangs, and has led ministry outreaches to numerous women on the Southside of Chicago who have fallen into lives of prostitution and drug abuse. Father Pfleger has personally challenged numerous drug dealers and conducted nonviolent marches for almost twenty years on Friday nights in the summer. He also led a multitude of in-your-face social justice missions to close down drug houses or hotels encouraging prostitution. When Father Mike arrived in the neighborhood in the early 1970s, there was rampant drug dealing, homelessness, and prostitution all around the walls of the church, whose attendance was down to fewer than 100 people. Today his church community is vibrant, thriving, and passionately full of life.

Father Pfleger with NBA basketball great Isiah Thomas speaking to his community about nonviolent change, while planting seeds of hope.

Mike Pfleger is a great demonstrator of vision, core values, co-creation strategy, and he uses influencers to support his mission. Whether it's his church community, the press, congressmen, local aldermen, or the mayor of Chicago, Mike Pfleger gains the support of people of influence in his community prior to going after social injustice.

Father Mike Pfleger understands the power of harnessing influencers to create change.

TELLING STORIES—YOUR STORIES

Persuasive individuals who are successful in the *long term* understand the power of setting a positive atmosphere in social or business situations. They have an outward focus and create authentic experiences through stories, which transform people from being critics to participants.

Concrete and vivid stories exert extraordinary influence because they transport people out of the role of critic into the role of participant. The more vibrant and relevant the story, the more the listener moves from thinking about the inherent arguments to experiencing every element of the tale itself.[10]

When this atmosphere is set, powerful things can happen. Whether this is good theatre or just perceptive interpersonal communication, the end result is the same. I have seen for twenty years how dark horse organizations enlist business evangelists to their organizations.

The following are some of the ways that the best dark horses unleash their fans, spreading the word about their products.

We are finding that the best dark horse companies understand the importance of building their company and image through others who

have influence. That's why social media is the most effective and efficient investment an organization can undertake, as long as it naturally flows out of the identity of the company.

INFLUENCERS ACCELERATE THE DEVELOPMENT OF AN "OPT-IN" COMMUNITY

Dark horse companies encourage their trusted customers and influencers to tell others about their positive brand experience and they look for unique means of providing new brand experiences.

This can include:

- » PARTNERING WITH SIMILAR BRANDS
- » SHARING NEW RESEARCH
- » OFFERING SAMPLING OPPORTUNITIES
- » INSPIRING BLOGGERS AND SOCIAL MEDIA USERS
- » ENCOURAGING INFLUENCERS
- » EDUCATING CONSUMERS VERSUS SELLING
- » PUBLISHING RELEVANT ARTICLES
- » LEADING PHILANTHROPIC EFFORTS TYING TO THEIR BRAND

As of the end of 2011, there were in excess of 170 million active blogs, not to mention Twitter, influencing business, culture, and individuals like you and me. The dynamic advantage of doing business today is that through the internet and social media, you have the potential to serve micro-consumer segments and influence influencers with unique interests. Most bloggers and Twitter users are educated, technologically savvy, and love to influence their network. That is why they are so special and valuable to all of us.

Pick your influencers carefully; choose those with like minds and vision… then let *them* tell your story. And, as I shared earlier, they can't be bought, only influenced.

Clearly, the dark horse must think differently when it comes to awareness building strategies—it is do or die. Ridderstråle and Nordström remind us all in *Funky Business Forever* that in an age of abundance, companies have to work hard to get noticed. Companies are competing for a few seconds of attention in a tidal wave of information hitting everyone, everywhere, all the time. If you want to attract potential customers and/or employees, you need to provide experiences that are immediate, intense, and instant. In an excess economy, attention is scarce. Handle it with care. [11]

AIRBORNE
EFFECTIVE FANS AND INFLUENCERS

Airborne is an over-the-counter supplement containing herbal extracts, vitamins, and other ingredients positioned as a supplement that supports the immune system.

The brand was introduced in 1997 by substitute teacher Victoria Knight-McDowell and marketed by co-founder Rider McDowell. The game changed in mid-December 2004 when Oprah Winfrey endorsed the herbal remedy, creating a tidal wave of positive awareness and dramatic out-of-stocks at many of the top retailers carrying Airborne. [12]

The brand had been tripling in sales each year since its inception, but the year of the Oprah endorsement brought sevenfold growth! Over the years, Airborne has been sold multiple times; in April 2012 the brand was sold for a cool $150 million in cash, and the brand is still at the beginning stages of growth.

Oprah was the ultimate brand influencer; her support changed the game for Airborne and the company.

INFLUENCERS MATTER

One of the things that dark horse companies do differently is work with influencers better than most. Their passion and company cause allows them to recruit new ambassadors of their brand through everyday conversations. There are four companies that come to mind who effectively used influencers to help build their brands.

Carma Labs is at the forefront of social media, with a rich database of fans who are informed of upcoming innovations, contests, and unique promotions. Carma Labs also gathers trend information from their top customers with online concept testing. [13]

Carmex is in an ongoing digital relationship with their consumers and influencers, utilizing blogs, consumer contests, and concept tests

GOJO worked very closely with the Center for Disease Control (CDC) on new health care guidelines advocating that hand sanitizers be incorporated into health care facilities to reduce hospital-acquired infections.

Ricola's natural cough drops attract celebrity influencers such as Mariah Carey, Christina Aguilera, Placido Domingo, Meatloaf, Michelle Pfeiffer, and Cate Blanchett, all of whom have spoken favorably of the brand.

Beiersdorf's therapeutic skin care brand Eucerin has developed great support by leading dermatologists and skin care experts who serve as advocates of the brand.

INFLUENCERS ON THE INSIDE: HIRE PLAYMAKERS

Great organizations are adept at collaborating with outside influencers while being skillful at hiring influencers who reside within the four walls of their offices. They hire playmakers!

We are now all participating in the *talent economy.* The top companies understand that you must attract talented, committed employees to create sustainable advantage. Similar to athletics and the arts, businesses are always in the mode of looking for talented playmakers—people who disrupt the flow of the game through ideas, relationships, or their competitive nature. These are individuals living in a constant state of never arriving. Their motivations include making a difference, working on relevant projects, and having the freedom to create.

Playmakers can be very disruptive because they are not satisfied with the status quo and are not content to do average work. These higher performers see the world through the lens of potential, which makes them very valuable. Their aspirations pull them forward and raise everyone's performance around them.

In today's economy, you are only as good as the diversity of your top talent and partners. The game is to associate and collaborate with talented people who really do think differently and provide unique value to your organization.

Dark horse companies are also committed to change and variation; they adjust to their environment as expectations and customer needs change. They are committed to a culture of mutation, holding on loosely to their strategy while adapting to opportunities and challenges that come their way. The only things that remain sacred and unchangeable are their core values. This adaptable mentality allows dark horse companies to deliver the best thinking and to serve up new corporate resources (human and material) in support of each customer initiative. Dark horse leaders realize that ongoing success only comes through zealous talent.

THE CONTAINER STORE
HIRING INFLUENCERS

Hiring great talent matters—just ask The Container Store, which sells containers, plastic organizers, and shelving. The company has been recognized for years as one of *Fortune Magazine*'s best places to work inAmerica. That's because their policy is to hire not just good people, but great people. They believe that one great person equals three good people.

The Apple culture under Steve Jobs believed that the best talent would deliver game changing performance. Jobs believed that hiring A-class talent (i.e., playmakers) could mean fifty or a hundred times the performance of a B or C player.

Game changing, talented playmakers serve as influencers both inside and outside of your organization. They carry the company cause and mission.

STRATEGIC INFLUENCE

One of the greatest values small organizations can offer top talent— in any industry—is the opportunity to design a business life which is inspirational, whether it be where an individual lives or how they contribute to a company's vision. The nature of larger firms many times precludes this from happening. For example, one of the challenges that many people struggle with in larger firms is that if you are not able to relocate to the head office, you hit a career roadblock; that's just the political dynamic of advancing in larger firms.

This means that dark horse companies can move up their competitive advantage both in talent acquisition and market share. Virtual jobs may not be the optimal arrangement for companies, but they do provide compelling opportunities for talent that wants to be a part of a special company's culture. I recognize that at first blush this seems to go against all principles of customer intimacy, but an individual's talent, curiosity, passion, tenacity, and cultural fit are much more valuable than the location of their residence.

The best dark horse organizations create peak performing virtual organization sourcing the brightest, the best, and the most passionate workers. These people are not hired help; they are your organization! They understand how attractive it is to position and market the organization as an interesting, eclectic place to work. Highly collaborative, loosely networked organizations are exhilarating to work for and with, and they inspire and attract the best of the best.

WHAT DOES YOUR TEAM OF INFLUENCERS LOOK LIKE?

INSIGHTS ON INFLUENCERS

» WE'RE ALL AFFECTED BY INFLUENCERS—EITHER PEOPLE WE TRUST, OR PEOPLE WE DON'T KNOW PERSONALLY BUT WHO IMPACT US FROM AFAR.

» OPINION LEADERS SET THE TONE FOR WHETHER IDEAS ARE ACCEPTED, OR WHETHER THEY ARE SHORT-LIVED AND DIE ON THE VINE.

» THE GREAT PERSUADER IS PERSONAL EXPERIENCE. WITH PERSISTENT PROBLEMS IT'S BEST TO HELP PEOPLE EXPERIENCE THE WORLD AS YOU EXPERIENCE IT.

» THE BEST EMOTIONAL BRANDS ARE NOT JUST SEEN, BUT *FELT DEEPLY*. IT'S ABOUT GAINING SHARE OF MIND, SHARE OF EMOTION, SHARE OF IMAGINATION, AND SHARE OF DREAMS.

» DARK HORSE COMPANIES DON'T NEED LOYALTY PROGRAMS BECAUSE THEY HAVE MORE THAN A BRAND COMMUNITY ON THEIR SIDE; THEY HAVE BELIEVERS.

» CONCRETE AND VIVID STORIES EXERT EXTRAORDINARY INFLUENCE BECAUSE THEY TRANSPORT PEOPLE OUT OF THE ROLE OF CRITIC INTO THE ROLE OF PARTICIPANT.

» DARK HORSE COMPANIES ARE ALSO COMMITTED TO CHANGE AND VARIATION; THEY ADJUST TO THEIR ENVIRONMENT AS EXPECTATIONS AND CUSTOMER NEEDS CHANGE. THEY ARE DEVOTED TO A CULTURE OF MUTATION BASED ON EMERGING COMPETITIVE OR CUSTOMER INSIGHTS.

THOUGHT STARTERS

1. WHAT INFLUENTIAL PEOPLE OR BRANDS SHOULD YOU INTRODUCE TO YOUR BRAND?

2. DO YOU KNOW OF ANY PASSIONATE PLAYMAKERS WHO WANT TO JOIN YOUR TEAM?

3. CAN YOU CO-BRAND OR BUILD ALLIANCES WITH OTHER COMPLEMENTARY COMPANIES THAT CREATE PRODUCTS YOUR CUSTOMERS ALREADY PURCHASE?

4. HOW CAN YOU PROVIDE MEANINGFUL SAMPLING OCCASIONS OR MAKE PRODUCTS EASY FOR CONSUMERS TO PASS ON TO THEIR FRIENDS OR RELATIVES?

5. HOW CAN YOU MOTIVATE YOUR TOP CUSTOMERS TO SHARE THEIR POSITIVE IMPRESSIONS OF YOUR COMPANY?

6. HOW CAN YOU UTILIZE RELEVANT SOCIAL NETWORKS TO HELP CREATE NEW ACCESS TO YOUR COMPANY?

7. WHAT PHILANTHROPIC CAUSES NATURALLY TIE TO YOUR BRAND AND CONNECT WITH YOUR COMPANY VALUES?

8. CAN YOU BRING A MORE PERSONAL, EMOTIONAL, OR EVEN FASHIONABLE COMPONENT TO YOUR PRODUCT OR SERVICE?

Chapter 8:

AGILITY
EMBRACING PARADOX

Most of us were raised to believe that messiness is out of order and should be avoided at all costs. But many dark horse organizations understand that corporate vitality is a byproduct of flexible, nimble—sometimes even *messy*—corporate cultures. Leaders uncomfortable with this type of culture are missing out on a big opportunity to win.

In *Surfing the Edge of Chaos*, authors Richard Pascale, Mark Millemann, and Linda Gioja discuss how complexity in nature is vital for growth. Think about how their principles (listed below) can be applied to your business:

» EQUILIBRIUM IS THE PRECURSOR TO DEATH. WHEN A LIVING SYSTEM IS IN A STATE OF EQUILIBRIUM, IT IS LESS RESPONSIVE TO CHANGES OCCURRING AROUND IT. THIS PLACES IT AT MAXIMUM RISK.

» IN THE FACE OF THREAT, LIVING THINGS MOVE TOWARD THE EDGE OF CHAOS. THIS CONDITION EVOKES HIGHER LEVELS OF MUTATION AND EXPERIMENTATION.

» WHEN THIS EXCITATION TAKES PLACE, THE COMPONENTS OF LIVING SYSTEMS SELF-ORGANIZE, AND NEW FORMS AND REPERTOIRES EMERGE FROM THE TURMOIL.

» LIVING SYSTEMS CANNOT BE DIRECTED ALONG A LINEAR PATH. UNFORESEEN CONSEQUENCES ARE INEVITABLE. THE CHALLENGE IS TO DISTURB THEM IN A MANNER THAT APPROXIMATES THE DESIRED OUTCOME.[1]

The authors believe these four principles invigorate all living systems, including organizations, and allow for mutation, adaptation, growth, and potentially, transformation.

Disruption is an agent of change.

As a dark horse company with agility, you are special and dangerous to competitors. You recognize that sustainable success is the result of uncovering and seizing new opportunities faster than your peers do. Although a messy business model can be very demanding, and at times stressful, it provides a differentiated and winning formula and allows for trial and error which leads to innovation and growth.

Here are two quick examples of using agility as a secret weapon for growth and advancement.

NOW FOODS
REFLEX REACTION TO DR. OZ

Dan Richard, the national sales manager of NOW Foods, shared with me a recent example of speed and agility by his dark horse company. In 2012, TV host Dr. Oz (a mainstream media influencer shot to stardom by mega-influencer Oprah Winfrey) spoke of the health benefits of taking 7-Keto-DHEA as an abdominal weight-loss supplement. NOW Foods has an employee monitor popular shows like Dr. Oz, so they got the news quickly. Their internal buying team immediately went out and purchased more than a year's worth of the key ingredients necessary to produce, pack, and ship 7-Keto-DHEA. NOW Foods went on to sell more than two years' worth of 7-Keto-DHEA in just two weeks![2]

An agile business culture—one unafraid of being messy—can seize new business opportunities and turn them into cash while differentiating from the pack. *Do you dare?*

DenTek Oral Care, another dark horse company mentioned earlier in this book, has shared with me that it isn't that they like winning; rather, they *hate losing.* The DenTek leader reminded me that the brand essence of their company, birthed by founder and former CEO John Jansheski, was to innovate or die. That is a serious commitment to flexibility and continuous improvement, and you cannot get there without a lot of messy activity.

The DenTek leader told me that employees were given the mandate to reinvent themselves every day. When you live this way, as uneasy as it may seem, you never have to worry about reinventing your company; it happens seamlessly and organically.[3]

My organization leads an executive share group called The Elevation Forum that meet four times a year and attracts sales and marketing executives from many of the top companies in the world of health, beauty, and wellness. The Elevation Forum is a place where the top retail merchants from many of the largest drugstore chains, club stores, and mass merchants in America share innovation and leadership ideas with other noncompetitive manufacturers of health and wellness products.

In this safe haven, executives get real about their business challenges, leadership issues, and the pressures of competing against organizations that are, in some cases, many times larger.

What are the common themes I see in companies that outperform larger competitors?

The Elevation Forum is an executive think tank where senior sales and marketing leaders discuss the emerging trends affecting their business. Many insights in this book have been uncovered in these groups.

LOVING PARADOX

The dark horse company walks in the paradox of being deeply systematic and serious about their brand and corporate identity—all the while being playful and agile.

Everyone in manufacturing, marketing, and all internal support areas in a dark horse company recognizes that the cultural attribute of flexibility helps them seize opportunities their competitors cannot. Everyone understands that *speed* is a competitive advantage, and it must be accompanied with candid communication to assess internal problems quickly and effectively. Only well-aligned teams can afford to use speed as a differentiator.

So, what should be the goal of smaller organizations? As Richard D'Aveni shares in his book *Hypercompetition*, the goal is to create "an active strategy of disrupting the status quo to create an unsustainable series of competitive advantages."[4] But shouldn't we want to *sustain* competitive advantages?

We live in a world where even if you create a breakthrough idea, within months someone is working around your patent and designing a similar (maybe better or cheaper) innovation. Dark horse companies know this, which is why they create and launch an item and immediately move into product redesign mode. Today we are all operating in a sphere of unsustainable advantage; that's what keeps innovation alive!

PRODUCTS FAIL IF PEOPLE DON'T GET TO TRY THEM

Each week, more than 100 million people walk through the doors of a Wal-Mart or Target store. Most Americans shop at these two powerful retailers at some point throughout the year. That's why the best companies use these strategic retailers (and others) as advocates of their brands. The mass merchandisers offer them very visible display activity, sampling, and secondary brand placement, representing millions of consumer impressions and marketing touches.

Retail and shopping expert Paco Underhill provides some powerful validation on the value of in-store consumer marketing. He states, "Close to 90 percent of all new products fail, but it isn't because people didn't like them—it's because *people never tried them*."[5] That's a humbling insight relevant to any business; all new products or services need a trial. Larger brands are given great display space in most retail stores because the consumer is often hunting for those brands specifically, which increases the potential of converting to a purchase. On the other hand, smaller companies and lesser known brands, because they have limited consumer demand, end up with less preferential display or shelf placement, but that's no reason to give up on getting your share of in-store visibility.

Crafty dark horse companies use customization as their strategy to gain shelf space; they design unique or exclusive products and/or promotional programs for top retail partners. This model of business allows the retailer to offer unique solutions to their consumers, encouraging stronger loyalty and a reason to shop exclusively at the store. Companies will change product configuration, add carrying cases and/ or smaller versions of the brand, or hold co-branding events with likeminded companies to improve awareness and trial.

The PURELL Jelly Wrap is a special custom item that encourages on-the-go usage and attaches to key chains, book bags, or briefcases.

PURELL JELLY WRAP
FROM CLEANING PRODUCT TO LIFESTYLE SOLUTION

We've talked in this book about GOJO Industries, makers of PURELL, the first hand sanitizer for the general public. For years, the company has utilized small bottle sampling events, co-branding efforts with other cough and cold brands, and lifestyle packs for people on the go. One such device, the PURELL Jelly Wrap, serves as a built-in marketing tool to encourage usage.

The PURELL Jelly Wrap is one of those clever strategies used to create meaningful brand awareness and consumer trial. What new parent wouldn't want one of these items connected to their key chains or the strap of their diaper bag? It is a clever means of encouraging new usage occasions, and a brilliant way of transforming a base cleaning product into a lifestyle solution.

GUM SOFT-PICKS
A SECONDARY LOCATION BRAND

Other emerging companies have applied the portable product strategy effectively in their awareness building campaigns. Sunstar Americas, marketer of the GUM oral care brand, created a unique little item most people have never heard of, but beloved by those who have. The item is the GUM Soft-Pick—a patented oral care device that removes plaque and food particles and is a convenient way to keep your teeth and gums healthy.

Sunstar has configured this item into multiple pack sizes with a special portable carrying case to help create visibility, awareness, and the potential for multiple store location placements

Sunstar's GUM Soft-Picks are an example of a brand built for secondary location due to its lifestyle qualities.

so consumers can be introduced to the item. These lifestyle packs are a great example of transforming a product stocked in the bathroom into an item incorporated into a consumer's daily routine. So why don't most companies go this portable lifestyle route with their products?

As most large public companies can tell you, profit margins reign supreme. When companies start introducing innovations such as short-run promotional packs, the marketing and manufacturing team's blood pressure begins to rise while the profit per unit begins to fall—never a good combination for effective corporate morale.

On the other hand, these agile activities are a way of life for dark horse companies—a vital means to continuing success with consumers. They understand that, in a world of consumer noise where decisions are often made in-store, this type of promotional pack design can be the spark to creating consumer awareness and brand trial.

APOLLO HEALTH AND BEAUTY
SPEED MEETS QUALITY

I spoke with Charles Wachsberg, President and Chief Executive of Apollo Health and Beauty which creates private brand offerings for many top health and wellness retailers in North America. "We have a huge focus on speed and agility, and the reason we can deliver on that promise is that our business mode and facilities are built to meet the customized needs of our cherished clients," says Wachsberg. "Our DNA of only designing custom products that resonate and are relevant puts us in a unique place on the competitive map. I don't believe that distinct quality and speed oppose each other. Since our clients demand both qualities, we will deliver on that expectation as the industry leader and custodian." [6]

True, this level of customization can create manufacturing tension, inventory challenges, and short-term inefficiencies due to short runs. But the pay-off is a dramatic expansion in consumer awareness, as well as deeper relationships with retail partners who serve as brand advocates.

Paco Underhill reminds us that we are all influenced by other people of influence. "Another reason touch-and-trial has become so important is the waning power of product brand names. When consumers believed in the companies behind the big brands, that belief went a long way toward selling things. Now we're all individualists... We'll believe it when we see/smell/touch/hear/taste/try it." [7]

Underhill's research underscores the importance of connecting intimately with customers in a live environment, whether you have a multimillion-dollar advertising campaign supporting your product or not. Grassroots in-store marketing activities, display programs, co-branding efforts, secondary brand placements, and other marketing strategies can build consumer brand support and valuable trial.

FAST PROTOTYPING

Dark horse companies often focus on being the hunter versus the hunted, releasing custom or new products that drive the competition to change direction. They focus on disrupting their competitors by creating quick custom innovation through fast prototyping.

Fast prototyping allows winning companies to test ideas very quickly while not damaging their core brand identity. It leaves their consumers or retail partners with the impression of flexibility, intimacy, and creativity. We have seen companies differentiate themselves by designing and modifying their base product to align with the consumer's lifestyle, allowing them to shelve the same formulation in multiple store locations under different positioning, package configurations, or secondary brand positioning.

Leading companies also use fast prototypes to probe the market with new formulations, delivery systems on a regional or local scale, or even with a limited panel of customers. This flexibility allows the brand to build valuable shelf presence with a short list of customers who served as advocates of the brand.

PERFECTION

Most people have had an idea or two they felt could be commercialized or launched as a new product idea. That is part of the genius of humans—we are meant to create, and we thrive on advancement and innovation. So why do so few of us take action and bring those thoughts to fruition?

The answer is that each of us, like companies, either gets bogged down focusing on other projects, lacks the courage to move forward, or works on perfecting the idea before taking it to the prototype stage. In other words, we let perfection rule the day, and we end up distracted—and someone else capitalizes on the idea.

Ideas travel, and they travel fast!

THE WAITING GAME

The best entrepreneurs recognize that being first with a good product is often more valuable than being second with a better idea. First to market is often a huge strategic advantage and must be acted upon—but not in all situations.

Reality is complicated; market opportunities are constantly opening and closing. A hit idea at one point could have been a dud a year earlier, or a yawning "me too" idea a year later. It's tough—likely impossible—to pinpoint the best moment to enter a market, but common sense dictates that new entrepreneurs can improve their odds if they weigh how much they stand to gain or lose by waiting.

According to Moren Levesque, an entrepreneurship researcher at the University of Waterloo, an indicator on whether to wait or enter a market first can be decided, at least in part, by finding out how hostile the learning environment is—that is, how much entrepreneurs can learn by observing other players *before* they launch, compared to what they learn from participating in the market *after* they launch.

Levesque, along with professors Maria Minniti of Southern Methodist University, and Dean Shepherd of Indiana University, used a mathematical model to weigh the risks and benefits of entering the market early. Their research, published in March 2006 in *Entrepreneurship Theory and Practice*, is among the first to explore "how different learning environments may influence the entry behavior of entrepreneurs."

The crux of the academics' findings on timing is this:

> » IN A HOSTILE (COMPETITIVE) LEARNING ENVIRONMENT, ENTREPRENEURS GAIN RELATIVELY LITTLE BENEFIT FROM WATCHING OTHERS. FOR EXAMPLE, IF THE RELEVANT KNOWLEDGE IS PROTECTED INTELLECTUAL PROPERTY, STUDYING THE MARKET BEFORE ENTERING WOULDN'T YIELD MUCH ADVANTAGE. IN THESE SITUATIONS, THE TRADE-OFF FAVORS ENTERING EARLY.
> » IN LESS HOSTILE LEARNING ENVIRONMENTS, WHERE ENTREPRENEURS GAIN VALUABLE INFORMATION LIKELY TO INCREASE THEIR SUCCESS JUST BY WATCHING OTHER COMPANIES, COMPANIES BENEFIT FROM WAITING AND LEARNING LESSONS FROM EARLIER PLAYERS. [8]

When there is not much to learn, the winners calculate their risk, apply great strategy, use their insights, influencers, and assets—and let it rip! They launch products and services, but always know an improved next generation is right around the corner.

Apple has certainly demonstrated this enough times: Steve Jobs' innovations were not perfect, but they were *first*. Their slight imperfections allowed for a reason to have a next generation!

PERPETUAL GAME OF TAG

Most marketers in our society suffer from a "perpetual game of tag," a term coined by Harvard professor Youngme Moon. Most consumers are overwhelmed by dozens of products that look, sound, and feel the same. Moon writes that, at some point, the difference between products can become too incremental for category devotees to appreciate anymore. A lover of language may delight in synonyms, but it's hard for anyone to see the point in a hundred different ways to say the word "blue." [9]

To be clear, I am not an advocate of anarchy, nor do I believe that all forms of innovation and breakthrough must come through chaos. Order, precedence, and authority have a place and they are necessary for effectiveness and for health (both personal and professional). But boredom can kill a healthy man, and boring people can bury a brand or organization!

Moon talks about the importance of creating a brand that occasionally offends some people because it is not like everyone else. Companies that step away from the mainstream game of tag start to embrace differentiation. Many of the dark horse companies that outperform their bigger playmates in the market do so by refusing to play follow-the-leader. Dark horses create their own positions and fill consumer gaps quickly and with the support of their consumers.

It's easier for people to think differently if everyone is allowed to fail fast and explore openings, and if leadership injects new innovators into the work culture.

FACEBOOKING PRODUCT CHANGES

Winning organizations don't get stale; they question, encourage reflection, and constantly challenge their assumptions. The health products company Yes To Inc. has new product development plans directly linked to the requests of their customers in many cases. For example, early in the life of the brand Yes To Carrots Leave-in Conditioners, changes were made to packaging and positioning after intense Facebook discussions with brand zealots. [10]

The company's co-founder Ido Leffler says he personally spends an hour a day on Facebook listening to and sharing with core customers. Social media is notorious for being messy at times, with controversy and unpopular opinions, but it's also at the edge—where innovation lives.

Today you have to mix it up a bit to thrive in business.

How comfortable are you in the mess?

INSIGHTS ON AGILITY

» CORPORATE VITALITY IS A BY-PRODUCT OF NIMBLE AND SOMETIMES MESSY CORPORATE CULTURES.

» SUSTAINABLE SUCCESS IS THE RESULT OF UNCOVERING AND SEIZING NEW OPPORTUNITIES FASTER THAN YOUR PEERS. ALTHOUGH A MESSY BUSINESS MODEL CAN BE VERY DEMANDING AND AT TIMES STRESSFUL, IT PROVIDES A DIFFERENTIATED AND WINNING FORMULA.

» THE DARK HORSE COMPANY WALKS IN THE PARADOX OF BEING DEEPLY SYSTEMATIC AND SERIOUS ABOUT THEIR BRAND AND CORPORATE IDENTITY—ALL THE WHILE BEING PLAYFUL AND AGILE.

» A SWIFT BUSINESS CULTURE—ONE UNAFRAID OF BEING MESSY—CAN SEIZE NEW BUSINESS OPPORTUNITIES AND TURN THEM INTO CASH WHILE DIFFERENTIATING FROM THE PACK.

» CREATE TRIALS AT ALL COSTS, EVEN IF THEY'RE MESSY. CUSTOMIZATION IS THE STRATEGY OF CHOICE FOR DARK HORSE COMPANIES.

» DARK HORSE COMPANIES OFTEN FOCUS ON BEING THE HUNTER VERSUS THE HUNTED, RELEASING CUSTOM OR NEW PRODUCTS THAT DRIVE THE COMPETITION TO CHANGE DIRECTION, DISRUPTING THEIR COMPETITORS BY CREATING QUICK INNOVATION THROUGH FAST PROTOTYPING.

» MANY OF THE DARK HORSE COMPANIES THAT OUTPERFORM THEIR BIGGER PLAYMATES IN THE MARKET DO SO BY REFUSING TO PLAY FOLLOW-THE-LEADER.

THOUGHT STARTERS

1. ARE YOU COMFORTABLE WITH RUNNING AN AGILE COMPANY, AND HOW IS IT HINDERING YOUR GROWTH?

2. WHAT IS AMBIGUOUS ABOUT YOUR COMPANY, AND HOW MIGHT THAT SERVE YOU COMPETITIVELY?

3. HOW CAN YOU USE DISRUPTION AS A WINNING STRATEGY?

4. WHAT NEW BUSINESS IDEAS ARE YOU PROBING THAT COULD CHANGE THE GAME?

5. WHO IS ON THE FRINGE IN YOUR AREAS OF EXPERTISE THAT COULD CHANGE THE COURSE OF YOUR BUSINESS?

6. WHAT IS THE ONE THING YOU SHOULD GO AFTER RIGHT NOW—WHETHER YOU ARE READY OR NOT?

7. WHAT NEW COMPETITORS ARE ON THE FRINGE BUT COMING FAST?

8. WHAT NEW BUSINESS MODELS COULD DISRUPT YOUR BUSINESS?

Chapter 9:

SURF THE SOCIETAL SHIFT
THE POWER OF CONVERGENCE

I don't set trends. I just find out what they are and exploit them.

—DICK CLARK, AMERICAN BANDSTAND

During one of the executive forums I moderate called The Elevation Forum, I was struck by the comment of a participant: "Emerging societal shifts sneak up on you, surround you, and eventually become you." Our viewpoints are largely influenced by experiences and societal shifts—current trends as well as our one-on-one encounters with other people and many other factors. Thought leaders and the media are catalysts of change, and many people believe companies can also help assist in societal shifts.

In business, if you're not staying informed of trends occurring in current affairs, food, entertainment, fashion, theatre, music, health, and a long list of other dynamics, you'll likely wake up one day to see you've fallen into the hole of irrelevance!

For every Borders Books that lost societal influence and went out of business, there is a Whole Foods or Amazon that is intimately in tune with cultural trends and is influencing the very society they are observing. Natural selection within industry means organizations must adapt to their environment to avoid extinction.

THE COOL FACTOR IN BUSINESS

Marketers have to respond to fundamental sociological changes and expectations by coming out with new products, services, and messages that tap into the cool factor. The more you know about the real world and real people, the more you can predict people's desires and expectations. Imagination can really come to life in exciting and profitable ways when one is in sync with the expectations of the marketplace. [1]

Not many of us have the instinctual insights of futurist Faith Popcorn, nor the discipline and curiosity to predict culture. But history does leave clues, and the future is bubbling up and unfolding right before our eyes.

I recently moderated an industry leadership summit with many of the top retail executives in the health and wellness industry. A piece of informal research was shared with the audience that caused me to pause for a bit. The question asked of a group of consumers was, "What new item do you wish you could buy that currently does not exist?" The responses were varied, from flying cars to an adult onesie for work (now *that* is a consumer opportunity gap). Interestingly, three consumer themes came through:

The best dark horse companies understand the pulse of the consumer (stated and unstated), and set strategy that recognizes where the ball is going, not where it's been.

THE POWER OF CONVERGENCE

I lean towards the idea that societal shifts occur at the convergence of two points:

1. EMERGING TECHNOLOGIES THAT ENABLE OR TRANSFORM NEW CONSUMER BEHAVIORS
2. THE PURPOSEFUL ACTIONS AND MOMENTUM OF SOCIETAL INFLUENCERS AND THE CULTURE AT LARGE

There is a synergistic effect when organizations align with the momentum of the culture. Similar to swimming in a stream, the quicker you align with the direction of the current, the better positioned you are to move quickly along the water, enjoying the rapids. Organizations that align with societal shifts maximize business opportunities and move from being carried by the shift to being a catalyst energizing the shift.

NAPSTER
SOCIETAL TSUNAMI IN MUSIC

Most recently, we have seen this phenomenon in the recording industry and in the way music is being digitally delivered and marketed to the consumer. Prior to the cultural shift, consumers purchased their music in brick and mortar outlets. But the game changed as teenagers starting sharing their digital music, along the way creating ethical and legal debates around music swapping, online piracy, and the role of protecting artists' rights to their work.

In 1999, Napster capitalized on the emerging trend of young people sharing their MP3 music files. At one point, it was estimated that more than twenty-five million people shared their music within this parallel market until Napster was closed down in July 2001. [2]

Apple was watching the same cultural trend in music procurement, but they better understood the future in collaborating with the artists and the music industry. Born in January 2001, iTunes changed the rules of the game; music that was being passed along for free was now being purchased through this new digital system.

But the game has changed once again. Enter Pandora and Spotify. Pandora is a music recommendation service which offers music from multiple genres based on the user's previous music selections. Users provide feedback to the songs chosen, and the service creates custom music offerings based on each person's preferences. The business is driven by a subscription service and a royalty sharing model. There has been years of haggling over how profits are shared with the music artists, but this model maintains a place in the center of the music culture.

Spotify was launched in 2008 as a commercial music streaming service providing over 20 million people with access to 20 million songs based on a subscription model. The music can be shared by registered users through Facebook and Twitter. Users are able to access their friends' favorite music and playlists, and notifications will appear on Facebook alerting friends to the music and playlists they are currently listening to.

*Are you swimming against the current or allowing the momentum to take you downstream? In your industry, **what's next**?*

WHAT THE HECK HAPPENED TO BOTTLED WATER?

We have seen a similar consumer shift in the bottled water category. Did you ever think, twenty years ago, you would be purchasing cases of water for your own consumption? No, of course not; it was a non-category. But today, bottled water is an $11 billion mega-category!

A few years ago, your bottled water options were limited to a five-gallon bottle for your water cooler, a one-gallon jug for emergencies, and a few specialty mineral waters such as Perrier (hardly mainstream, especially in the United States). But today's bottled water options include:

- » PURIFIED WATER TREATED TO REMOVE CHEMICALS AND PATHOGENS;
- » SPRING WATER SOURCED FROM UNDERGROUND SPRINGS WHERE THE WATER FLOWS TO THE EARTH'S SURFACE;
- » MINERAL WATER COMING FROM UNDERGROUND SOURCES AND THAT HAS NOT BEEN PURIFIED;
- » ARTESIAN WATER FROM WELLS THAT TAPS AQUIFERS;
- » SPARKLING WATER WITH ADDED CARBON DIOXIDE;
- » DISTILLED WATER BOILED AND THEN RE-CONDENSED FROM THE STEAM THAT THE BOILING PRODUCES; AND
- » VITAMIN WATER, INFUSED WITH A VARIETY OF VITAMINS AND MINERALS.

The type and range of water options and brand positioning are diverse and expanding, but the real shift is the amount of bottled water the average consumer now purchases. According to the Beverage Marketing Corporation of New York, U.S. consumption reached a historical high of 9.1 billion gallons in 2011; per capita consumption peaked at 29.2 gallons, up from 18.2 gallons in 2001. [3]

What happened was that bottled water companies understood the power of convergence; they understood that wellness awareness and lifestyle shifts in the general public could dovetail nicely with their own water manufacturing and bottling innovations. Even the three largest beverage makers in the world—Coke, Pepsi, and Nestle—have invested in bottled water products.

Surfing a societal shift is smart business.

The discipline of mapping out and leading initiatives that align with upcoming societal shifts is part of a threefold process:

1. KEEP AN EYE ON EARLY ADOPTERS AND *FRINGE INNOVATORS* WHO CREATE NEW IDEAS OR WAYS OF THINKING.
2. BECOME A STUDENT OF CULTURE WHILE CONSISTENTLY LOOKING FOR PATTERNS; *CONNECT THE DOTS* BETWEEN DIFFERENT FACTORS IN SOCIETY AND BUSINESS CAPABILITIES.
3. ALWAYS *CHALLENGE* YOUR MENTAL MODELS AND ASSUMPTIONS.

THE FRINGE

The majority of new ideas do not come from the mainstream: they bubble up from fringe groups in society and within organizations, through alliance partners and a whole host of individuals who work a little (or a lot) outside of traditional norms.

» THEY ARE NOT CONFINED BY RULES.
» THEY DO NOT HAVE A PREDETERMINED, STRUCTURED WAY OF THINKING.
» THEY LOOK AT EVERYTHING WITH NEW EYES AND ASK, "WHY" AND "WHY NOT?"
» THEY DON'T RESIST CHANGE, BUT EMBRACE IT.
» THEY AREN'T AFRAID OF MAKING MISTAKES AND LEARNING FROM THEM.
» THEY ARE OPEN-MINDED, AND THEIR OPENNESS LETS THEM IMAGINE WHAT COULD BE.

The few can convert the many.

Here is a company attempting to take advantage and ride the wave of a number societal trends, including portability, purity of products, eco-friendliness, fun marketing communication, and lifestyle branding. Their name: Evolution of Smooth (EOS).

EOS
FEEL ME... SEE ME...

Everything about the startup company Evolution of Smooth (EOS)—from their ingredients and compelling packaging, to the irresistible feel and scent of their lotions, creams, and lip balms—is created to be pretty remarkable and remarkably pretty. Scott Pakula, Executive VP of Sales at EOS, says "Our brand meets the needs of today's women looking for products that both work great and look great, which is why our product line has such a beautiful design. We have slowly been building the brand first starting with lip balms, followed by shave creams and hand/ body lotions." [4]

The packaging of EOS screams "Pick me up!" with designs accentuating the softness of the brand and the smoothness of the formula. This is a real experiential brand that has the potential to connect on very emotional levels with their core consumers.

But how does a dark horse company like EOS compete in four categories dominated by some of the largest and strongest multinational consumer package-goods companies in the world?

Part of the answer is that EOS rides the wave of three societal trends building their brand:

» CONSUMERS WANT GREAT PRODUCTS THAT WORK, BUT ARE ALSO BEAUTIFULLY DESIGNED; HOW THINGS LOOK ON YOUR BATHROOM COUNTER MATTERS TODAY.

» CONSUMERS WANT PRODUCTS THAT ARE POSITIONED AS NATURAL (FREE OF CHEMICALS) WITHOUT FEELING CLINICAL.

» ALL CONSUMERS—IN PARTICULAR FEMALE TEENS, TWEENS, AND YOUNGER WOMEN—ARE LOOKING FOR FUN, HIGH-END BEAUTY PRODUCTS AT A GREAT PRICE.

Evolution of Smooth (EOS)—an experiential brand that blends natural ingredients, unique packaging designs, and engaging fragrances and scents.

As EOS broadens their line, consumers will more than likely follow because of the sense of feel and high touch the brand brings to their world.

GOJO
BETTER TO TREND TOO SOON THAN TOO LATE

GOJO Industries formally dedicates leaders within the organization to monitor and stay in front of social, cultural, and international societal shifts. "You need to see the trend before it pays off," says CEO

Joe Kanfer. "We keep ideas and trends in the conversation whether they pay off now or not."

In the early 1980s, Kanfer was watching a trend in the hospital segment: the use of liquid body washes at many facilities. After much research, GOJO created and regionally marketed the first liquid body soap product sold at retail. The brand, designed for consumers, was called Shower Up—and it failed miserably within the first year, according to Kanfer. The lesson he learned with this limited launch was that he was years ahead of a consumer trend that was not ready to be commercialized. (Their liquid body soap products are still sold today in their professional soap division.)

Less than a decade later, Kanfer was evaluating another professional trend—the use of waterless soap products (hand sanitizers) in restaurants and hospitals. This time he hit the societal wave at the perfect point. As Kanfer says, watching cultural trends is an art form, and it is very easy to be too late and even too early. Dark horse companies marry great product with beautiful design that is perfect for their consumers at the *perfect time.* [5]

CONNECTING THE DOTS

There are tremors occurring every day in the form of new consumer trends, societal movements, and social causes. Ideas are percolating all around us. Each of these data points independently may not mean a lot, but once you stand back and see them in context, the landscape looks very different. Few in our hectic lives take the time to broadly scan all facets of our culture and then connect the dots, finding out how we got to the place where:

» HAND SANITIZERS BECAME MAINSTREAM, REPLACING SOAP AND WATER IN HOSPITALS

» WATER WAS SOMETHING TO PURCHASE IN BOTTLES

» ORGANIC PRODUCTS ARE NO LONGER JUST PURCHASED BY ENVIRONMENTALISTS

And even if we can figure how those societal trends happened, that's easy compared to connecting the dots *going forward*. What marketer or product development person wouldn't love to have a crystal ball! Having skills in forecasting and prognostication can position companies for success where most others fail. Dark horse companies are engaged with the larger trends and are busy working at meeting future needs in a work culture that emphasizes listening and active imaginations while looking for new dots to connect.

Dark horse companies are always (almost neurotically) checking and re-checking their current assumptions to see if things have changed. This is part of their formula for eliminating blind spots or competitive hijackings.

What follows are two last examples of emerging dark horses that surf societal shifts toward success.

SUNDIAL BRANDS
THE INCLUSIVE BRAND

Retailing strategies have always been about exclusion, including sorting products by color and pricing segments and sorting shoppers by age, income, and even skin color. "The beauty aisle is where segregation still is legal," laughs Sundial Brands CEO and co-founder Richelieu (Rich) Dennis. "We hope to eliminate that soon. Our whole brand identity and purpose is about inclusion. You don't know what you are missing when you exclude others."

Sundial Brands, makers of Shea Moisture and Nubian Heritage personal care, is a family run operation filled with purpose and passion. They are rich in identity, with a special hidden asset of a diverse group of passionate employees who play big and are not afraid of failure. They believe they can change the world by creating a company that lives and breathes inclusiveness. Both the products and the company stress inclusion of all races, views, and skin conditions—and the changing U.S. consumer is looking for products and companies that both respect and include them in the conversation.

Sundial Brands was founded in 1992 by Rich Dennis and Nyema Tubman, former college roommates who created an assortment of high quality, eco-friendly natural skin care products which support local communities and fair trade around the world. This unique upstart began with Dennis selling a select group of products on the streets of Harlem twenty years ago to a brand challenging many of the top specialty soaps, lotions, and shampoos in the market today. They made the products in their apartments and tested and sold the items on the streets, working like a laboratory to better understand the customer and eventually nurturing a cult following behind their unique oils, lotions, and Shea butters. So how does a company with limited resources crack through the very competitive business of natural skin care?

From the Streets of Harlem to the Shelves of Walgreens, CVS, and Target, Sundial Brands is a brand inclusive of everyone.

As Richelieu shared with me, "I knew we had something in college when my mom would send a group of products that she and my grandmother had been making and selling in the village markets. My friends loved the items. The unique product formulas were created by my grandmother after she gathered unique nuts and oils back in Liberia, Africa."

His relationship with his mom framed his thinking about people, business, and life in general. "She taught me that compassion and protecting your personal legacy, including how you engage with others, must guide your life. I am guided by a focus on compassion, thoughtfulness, and I am not afraid of risk and failure. I am not afraid of anything," he continued, "because of what I saw as a child. We lived through a ten year civil war, where I lost friends and watched other villages decimated as I walked home from school."

Dennis stated that they create products and provide education that addresses a consumer group he refers to as the "New General Market." Sundial Brands has deep cultural competence recognizing that African-Americans, Latinos, and other minorities account for over 50 percent of all births in the U.S., and that by 2040, the non-Caucasian population will equal the Caucasian population. This growth part of the economy is also the least understood.

This is the community that supports his products and his larger vision of finding commonality in each other. He is building a following attracted to his products and the larger vision of inclusion. Rich shared,

In a market saturated by Starbucks, how does Joe Coffee do it? Jonathan Rubinstein believes it's the experience.

"All people want to feel included and want the same things in life. My job is to unite people, to create inclusion around what we all value. It is not about the creating healthy skin care products. It's about the heart. The product line is the pay-off of the larger course we are charting."

Dennis has built a dark horse brand through inclusion and brand experience. Sundial understands that the culture is shifting, and that to thrive, you must purposefully shift and include consumers on their own terms.

JOE COFFEE
ART + COMMUNITY + EDUCATION

How do you take a saturated market and make it your own? Ask Jonathan Rubinstein, founder of Joe Coffee in New York City. His gourmet coffee-shop business started in the West Village in 2003, and has grown to ten NYC stores (including Grand Central, Union Square, the West Village, Brooklyn, and Columbia University) and a move into Philadelphia in the near future.

It is estimated that the island of Manhattan alone has almost 200 Starbucks coffee shops, and the surrounding community has almost 700 community coffee shops. With that level of market penetration, what is contributing to this dark horse company's success?

The answer: Joe Coffee is surfing the societal shift towards:

» INTIMACY: THE COFFEE BAR VS. THE COFFEE CHAIN STORE.
» SMALLER STORE FOOTPRINT: TYING INTO THE ECO-CONSCIOUS MOVEMENT.
» NON-INTRUSIVE DESIGN OF ARCHITECTURE: FITS INTO THE NEIGHBORHOOD LANDSCAPE, UNLIKE NATIONAL COFFEE RETAILERS SHOUTING THEIR LOGO AND COLORS.
» SENSUAL EXPERIENCE FOR THE FOODIE/COFFEE LOVER: HIGH-QUALITY COFFEE IS BEAUTIFULLY PRESENTED AS A WORK OF ART.
» PRODUCTS AS AN EXPERIENCE: COFFEE IS MORE THAN JUST A USEFUL, CONSUMABLE ITEM.
» PASSIONATE, ENGAGED EMPLOYEES: THE PUBLIC'S GROWING DEMAND FOR CUSTOMER SERVICE EXCELLENCE IS SATISFIED.
» COFFEE LOVERS' DESIRE TO BECOME BARISTAS THEMSELVES: SELF-IMPROVEMENT AND CONTINUING EDUCATION IS OFFERED IN-STORE.

Many Joe Coffee shops offer barista classes called Coffee Exploration, as well as gourmet coffee-making lessons. This organization has been recognized as having some the best-trained baristas around, and they share their passion in experiential classes.

A cup of coffee at Joe Coffee in New York is a work of art.

Similar to Whole Foods, the employees at Joe Coffee really make the difference. They want to be there, they enjoy making unique blends of coffee, and they like talking about their special products.

Rubinstein and his sister Gabrielle, who is also his business partner, have blended art, community, and education into a cup of coffee. Their formula for success includes staff who buy into the vision, distinct-tasting coffee which is beautifully presented to the patron, and a real connection with the neighborhood. [6]

Coffee is one of the most crowded, competitive categories in a retail store. And with over 700 New York community coffee shops crowding competitors out, how does a small family-run operation create a winning experience?

They understand how to optimize the emerging behaviors of higher end coffee consumers, the power of societal influencers, and distinct consumer experience.

How could they go wrong?

INSIGHTS ON SURFING THE SHIFT

» SOCIETAL SHIFTS OCCUR AT THE CONVERGENCE OF EMERGING TECHNOLOGIES AND THE MOMENTUM AND THE ACTIONS OF SOCIETAL INFLUENCERS.

» THE MORE YOU KNOW ABOUT THE REAL WORLD AND REAL PEOPLE, THE MORE YOU CAN PREDICT PEOPLE'S DESIRES AND EXPECTATIONS. IMAGINATION CAN REALLY COME TO LIFE IN EXCITING AND PROFITABLE WAYS WHEN ONE IS IN SYNC WITH THE MARKET.

» THE BEST DARK HORSE COMPANIES UNDERSTAND THE PULSE OF THE CONSUMER (STATED AND UNSTATED), AND SET STRATEGY THAT RECOGNIZES WHERE THE BALL IS GOING, NOT WHERE IT'S BEEN.

» ORGANIZATIONS THAT ALIGN WITH SOCIETAL SHIFTS MAXIMIZE BUSINESS OPPORTUNITIES AND MOVE FROM BEING CARRIED BY THE SHIFT TO BEING A CATALYST ENERGIZING THE SHIFT.

» THE MAJORITY OF NEW IDEAS DO NOT COME FROM THE MAINSTREAM; THEY BUBBLE UP FROM FRINGE GROUPS IN SOCIETY AND WITHIN ORGANIZATIONS, THROUGH ALLIANCE PARTNERS AND ALTERNATIVE STREAMS.

» ALIGNING WITH SOCIETAL SHIFTS REQUIRES WATCHING THE FRINGE, CONNECTING THE DOTS, AND CHALLENGING YOUR OWN ASSUMPTIONS; BRING NEW IDEAS TO EARLY ADOPTERS.

» DARK HORSE COMPANIES ARE ENGAGED WITH THE LARGER TRENDS AND ARE BUSY WORKING AT MEETING FUTURE NEEDS IN A WORK CULTURE THAT EMPHASIZES LIS-TENING AND ACTIVE IMAGINATIONS WHILE LOOKING FOR NEW DOTS TO CONNECT.

THOUGHT STARTERS

1. WHAT IS YOUR INTUITION TELLING YOU ABOUT YOUR ORGANIZATION AND THE FUTURE?

2. HOW COULD YOU CHANGE THE DIRECTION OF YOUR TEAM TO OPTIMIZE THE NEXT CULTURAL SHIFT?

3. WHAT TRENDS ARE YOU MONITORING TO ENSURE THAT YOU STAY IN FRONT OF YOUR INDUSTRY?

4. HAVE YOU HAD YOUR THREE MOST INNOVATIVE CUSTOMERS OUT FOR LUNCH LATELY TO DISCUSS FUTURE DESIGN NEEDS?

5. WHEN DO YOU PLAN ON CHANGING YOUR COMPENSATION SYSTEM TO REWARD OR RECOGNIZE INNOVATORS IN YOUR COMPANY?

6. WHAT COMPANY IN YOUR INDUSTRY WORKS ON THE FRINGE AND HAS A HISTORY OF UNDERSTANDING THE FUTURE?

7. WHAT CAN YOUR ORGANIZATION LEARN FROM THE EARLY ADOPTERS WITHIN YOUR BUSINESS? WHAT ARE THEY SAYING AND WHAT IS ON THEIR MINDS?

8. ARE YOU USING THIRD-PARTY ALLIANCES TO GAIN INSIGHTS INTO THE FUTURE?

Chapter 10:

A CULTURE OF GRACE

(Honorable Organizations)

Grace isn't a little prayer you chant before receiving a meal. It's a way to live.

—JACKIE WINDSPEAR, AUTHOR

I was twenty-two years old, fresh out of college, and giving a sales presentation to the fifty-year-old head buyer of a regional food chain in Western Michigan. My suit felt uncomfortable, my hands were sweaty, and there was tightness in my chest causing both my knees and voice to shake. I felt out of my element, and I felt ineffective.

This was my first big presentation during my first month of work at my first real job. I felt forced, robotic, and unnatural. To this day, I don't remember what I said to the buyer, but I know it was not effective. I was more worried about catching my breath and casually wiping the sweat from my forehead and temples than asking thought-provoking questions or discussing ideas that could be good for his business.

My objective for the meeting was to discuss a special promotion on a liquid bath line which our company marketed. I presented the promotional materials as if I was a twelve-year old reading a script for a holiday play. I walked out of this forty-five-minute meeting embarrassed and a wreck. My boss, who was three years older than I was but seemed much more my senior, put his arm around my shoulders and said, "Hey, I thought you were going to tear that presentation paper in half during the appointment. Just relax and you'll be fine." Smiling, he grabbed my shoulder even harder and said, "Seriously, Dan: don't worry."

His words of encouragement allowed grace to enter the room—dignified, accommodating, and generous—offering a reprieve for a sales meeting that fell apart. Grace earned my trust from that point on—and taught me about leadership and honor and patience. That moment galvanized my perspective on leadership, providing an insight into why some organizations are exceptional and why others fail. Cultures which are fueled by grace, are cultures which thrive because they call out the hidden gold buried in their associates.

GREAT ORGANIZATIONS BLEND TRUTH WITH GRACE

Great organizations and great leaders come in all styles: some bold and loud, others more restrained. Regardless, it is *trustworthy* leaders who retain their employees and get the most out of them. A blend of truth and grace unlocks organizational success.

Honesty without grace can damage organizational trust because it becomes over-critical. Grace without honesty is too soft and therefore fails to maintain high performance standards.

When any of us feel threatened, we move into a defensive mode, which limits long-term success. Grace is a gift we give our employees and ourselves; practice it, and your organizations will thrive.

TOMS
A CULTURE OF GRACE

During a trip to Argentina in 2006, entrepreneur Blake Mycoskie had a vision for helping to change the world through an innovative business, rather than another charity. His company, originally called Shoes for Tomorrow, was born after he came face to face with shoeless children living in extreme poverty.

In his further travels abroad with the company, now called Toms, Mycoskie was moved to learn of the health risks that children face from not wearing shoes. For example, the disfiguring disease known as mossy foot, a form of elephantiasis, can be minimized simply by wearing shoes.

I learned of Toms when I noticed a woman wearing a pair on an airplane; I asked her why she bought them and she said, "This is my way of helping to change the world." I was overwhelmed by the encounter, and by how business can be a catalyst for change. The woman didn't buy a pair of shoes; she had caught a vision.

Blake Mycoskie, founder of Toms, with some of the children who receive new shoes from his business model, One for One.

Here is how Mycoskie's One-for-One business model works: when a consumer purchases new shoes (and now eyewear, helping 150,000 people with vision problems), their investment funds an additional pair of new shoes or glasses for someone in dire need. More than ten million pairs of new shoes have been given to children in more than sixty third-world countries. The shoes, in various styles and made from recycled materials, are sold at high-end stores such as Nordstrom, Neiman Marcus, Whole Foods, and Urban Outfitters. [1]

Blake Mycoskie's decision to help underprivileged children goes beyond social entrepreneurship; it is *grace in action*.

GRACE IS A PARADOX

Charles Handy writes in *The Age of Paradox* that "to live with simultaneous opposites is, at first glance, a recipe for indecision at best, schizophrenia at worst. It need not be." [2] Business, like life, is about managing paradox and still maintaining your peace. And it includes extending grace while holding people accountable.

Handy gives some examples of paradoxes: "Parents are simultaneously tough and strict, tender and relaxed with their children. If they do it right, the kids understand. Organizations are tight and loose; concerned only about the longer term in some areas, but passionate about detail in others." [3]

Tom Peters and Bob Waterman speak of this idea of being "both loose and tight simultaneously" in their research of the top companies in their best-selling book *In Search of Excellence*. This idea rears its head again in the breakthrough work of Jim Collins in *Good to Great*. Collins' research states that the most sustainable organizations have an incredible, almost insatiable attention to detail (and ambition), but are governed by leaders who walk in humility and give their employees room to breathe.

Real leadership is the art of being *all in* with your vision, but holding on to that same vision with an open palm. This includes:

» BALANCING STRATEGY AND CREATION
» CONNECTING AUTHENTICALLY WITH PEOPLE

» FEARLESSLY DRIVING EXECUTION

» SYSTEMATIC PLANNING, THINKING, AND REFLECTING ON YOUR BUSINESS

These four quadrants don't normally exist symbiotically within each of us; at times they can even be at war with each other. But dark horse companies have learned to thrive in this ambiguity.

HIRE DIFFERENT; ENCOURAGE DISSENT

If you have an honest confidant in your life, you are both blessed and rare. All of us need objective "point people" we can turn to provide us with personal feedback and coaching. The best-run companies have such people either on staff, or as informal coaches who honestly provide performance insights to help illuminate the blind spots that limit their effectiveness. After all, an unchecked personal leadership flaw can lead everyone in the organization to an unhappy ending.

As a result, strive to hire diverse people and encourage dissent. It's not easy to deliberately hire people who are different, let alone invite their candid feedback on your leadership and the company's performance. Look past the results-driven résumé and consider hiring someone with offbeat interests, a track record of trying disruptive new things, someone unlike you. During the interview, probe deeply to see what kind of dissent you can get out of him or her. Invite contrarian thinking and discussion.

Not everyone must—or even should—think the same way for innovation to flourish in a company.

VIRTUAL BOARDS

It takes guts to surround yourself with advisors who make you a little uneasy, know more than you, and are blunt. I would love to say that I always invite counter opinions, but I don't. In the world of consulting, you diagnose problems, evaluate patterns, and recommend solutions to fix things. That's easy. Listening to opposition is not.

Getting direct feedback on how you can be better, or where you are personally failing, can be hard to hear—at first. But dark horses give and accept constructive feedback, the sole purpose of which is improvement.

Blair Kellison, president of Traditional Medicinals, told me his company has created an internal council which is comprised of the owner and senior leadership to ensure core beliefs and values are upheld. They also have an outer circle of management; if anyone in the company feels that corporate values or identity are at risk, they are asked to talk it over with the council. This takes a high degree of honesty and accountability, and a strong moral compass, with an emphasis on always doing the right thing.

The company is rarely governed or directed by the quarterly or annual sales targets. This does not mean that they do not have sales targets or that they are not monitored strictly. They do, but their values, product quality, passion for their consumer, and larger purpose will never be at risk due to short-term objectives or financials. [4]

SUCCESS IS NOT YOUR FRIEND

Let's face it: success and achievement can make you a little high on your own supply. As much as we don't want to hear this, success is *not* your friend. We strive for it, but it normally clouds our views and assessments.

I am reminded of three very powerful insights shared by Gary Hamel, author and founder of Strategos Consulting, at the 2011 National Association of Chain Drug Stores annual meeting. Hamel's keynote address focused on the characteristics of the agile corporation. The following are three ideas I am still pondering:

1. SEEK OUT CRITICS AND DISSIDENTS IN YOUR LIFE AND BUSINESS.
2. TRY TO CONSISTENTLY IMAGINE THE UNIMAGINABLE. CREATE RELEVANT CONTINGENCY PLANS THAT ADDRESS "WHAT HAPPENS IF..." TO PROACTIVELY PREPARE FOR UNPLANNED THREATS.
3. SPEND TIME ON THE EDGE OF YOUR INDUSTRY (WHERE NEW IDEAS ARE BEING BORN), OBSERVING CULTURAL TRENDS AND POTENTIAL COMPETITIVE DISRUPTIONS. TO CREATE THE FUTURE, YOU MUST UNDERSTAND THE FUTURE. [5]

Are you willing to open yourself up to that level of third-party coaching and assessment? Are you willing to go where the facts about your leadership take you?

ON BECOMING A LEADER: WISDOM FOR THE AGES

Warren Bennis, professor of Business Administration and chairman of the Leadership Institute at the University of Southern California's Marshall School of Business, provides a blueprint for leadership success. He has advised hundreds of CEOs and U.S. presidents while authoring numerous books on leadership and change management.

Yes, we are living in a virtual economy, underwritten by daunting technological advancements and fueled by the spirit of disruption, but the basics of leadership as communicated by Bennis are for the ages. His ideas are both timeless and necessary for today's emerging organizations.

In his book *On Becoming a Leader*, he provides fodder for innovation gurus of all types. I find it necessary to outline some of his best ideas because we find these qualities in the dark horses that sneak up and eventually outperform their larger competitors. He says great leaders:

» MASTER THE CONTEXT; THEY LISTEN TO THEIR INNER VOICE, LEARN FROM MENTORS, AND GIVE THEMSELVES OVER TO A GUIDING VISION.

» UNDERSTAND THAT WE ARE OUR OWN RAW MATERIAL; ONLY WHEN WE KNOW WHAT WE'RE MADE OF, AND WHAT WE WANT TO MAKE OF OURSELVES, CAN WE BEGIN OUR LIVES.

» HAVE SELF-KNOWLEDGE AND SELF-INVENTION.

» KNOW THEY NEED TO GET PEOPLE ON THEIR SIDE AND KEEP THEM THERE; GENERATING TRUST IS NO GAME, AND THE FORMULA DOESN'T COME IN A BOX. TRUST CEMENTS STRONG ORGANIZATIONS—WHEN YOU DON'T HAVE IT, YOU MUST RELY ON CONTROL.[6]

GIVING GRACE

Leaders that extend grace are transformational leaders. Grace creates an atmosphere of trust, service, and a provision that cannot be installed, purchased, or trained. It cannot be legislated, nor can it be regulated. It is a vision that must be caught and not bought. Dark horse companies get this; they do their best work in a culture that is threaded with grace—for employees, customers, partners, suppliers, and the community at large.

Rich Dennis of Sundial Brands reminds us that "great business is very personal; I have to personally connect with my customers so we can create together. I believe in getting to know them intimately. Our retailer partners are like family so we can create a special business. To become truly aligned, it doesn't happen with handshakes; oftentimes realness is unleashed through an embrace or a hug." He continues, "We attract very passionate and diverse people to our team. Our focus has always been on the community that we serve. Once the community understands our authenticity, we bring them into the fold. They go and share the love with others. It's not a technique; it's how we think and who we are."

GOJO Industries founder Jerry Lippman started with a simple but powerful moment of grace: free peanut butter and jelly, plus free bread, milk, and coffee for anyone, any time at his company. He believed he had a responsibility to ensure no one would ever start work hungry or go home hungry. The tradition still stands after decades.

Carma Labs believes that coaches coach and players play, but "we don't play scared," says Mike Pietsch, EVP, Sales and Marketing. "You are asked to create and execute and you always trust that everyone has each other's back; grace is given when mistakes are made."

Method Home Products co-founder Eric Ryan says, "Making soap never motivated us, but creating a culture which elevates work to a higher place of mission, now that inspires me."

derma e Natural Body Care "doesn't function on large egos or star performers," says president David Stearn. "We all believe in helping each other to get the job done… We give back to various local and international charities such as Special Olympics, Heal the Bay, The Polaris Project, The Paraguay Project, and World Wildlife Fund. Members of our team also volunteer regularly in the community and are rewarded for doing so."

Ricola president Bill Higgins says, "I believe trust is the residual effect of promises kept. I am very clear with our team to please hold me accountable to my commitments." Ricola also provides training on conflict management: "Vulnerability is important in all discussions," says Higgins.

Beiersdorf North America President and General Manager Bill Graham shares his mandate: "It's all about people and learning… We play differently than most companies because of the close collaboration we have across functions. Values play an important role in our company."

Wahl Home Products' Bruce Kramer believes leaders create the environment for others to win in. "We allow people to be stars. We encourage others to enjoy the glory of their success and carry the pride of ownership… but we emphasize joint accountability."

NOW Foods supports a number of initiatives including Vitamin Angel Alliance, Feeding America, Compassion International, World Relief, and Smile Train, to name a few. In twenty-five years, no one at NOW Foods has been fired, and to execute a firing takes three levels of signatures; it truly is a last resort. This is a company that is agile, collaborative, and inventive, while offering an on-site chaplain for employees.

Yes To Inc. co-founder Ido Leffler says there is a sign in the office that states, "Yes to ideas that stick!" That positivity pervades across the organization, which recently announced their partnership with Kenya-based non-profit Mama Hope to launch the Yes To Hope campaign to build micro farms across schools in Kenya and Tanzania. "I fully understand that businesses are in business to make a profit," says Leffler. "But a business is also platform to change culture and hopefully improve lives."

Tom Hurley, a good friend of mine, always reminds me that our gifts in business are to help change lives for the better. Tom is of Irish descent; he is six-feet tall, 170 pounds (with gusts to 185 during the grilling season), a practical joker, and a very charismatic leader in his community who can start a tent revival on a number of topics at the drop of a hat. His passions include anything having to do with racial reconciliation, social justice, and he encourages, mentors, and coaches people who have fallen on hard times. He works in a ministry on

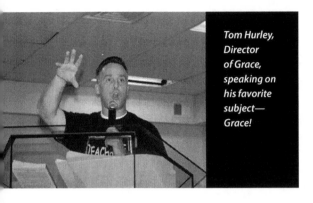

Tom Hurley,
Director
of Grace,
speaking on
his favorite
subject—
Grace!

the south-side of Chicago in a predominantly multicultural community.

When Tom was in his early twenties, he had two brain surgeries to remove a tumor that was causing a barrage of seizures and affecting the quality of his life and his outlook in general. As he has shared with me many times, he had been prepared to die, but was given the gift of life. After his second successful brain surgery, Tom was given a different vision of the purpose of his life. This second chance, as he describes it, has allowed Tom the ability to speak to and encourage the lives of the disenfranchised and ex-offenders.

Tom has worked for years in Chicago's south-side Englewood community—an area historically plagued by crime, violence, drug use, and unemployment—and his work includes high-risk parole and re-entry centers. Tom's personal mission has always focused on helping others find freedom from racism, their past, addictions, and areas of injustice that still plague underserved urban neighborhoods. He believes his purpose is to *show grace to others* by helping them understand their true identity and divine destiny, while helping them unleash their true gifts. If I had an opportunity to change the job title on his business card, I would call him Director of Grace.

The statistics show that 60 percent of ex-offenders reoffend and return to prison, but Tom and his ministry have been highly successful in turning those numbers around. Over a cup of coffee, he once told me, "Seeing men regain their life and their dignity gives me life."

Tom has always been unorthodox, and he leads this operation differently than most. In a criminal system where returning to prison is the norm, he sees his role as mentor, brother, and advocate for his clients' emotional and social health. Tom has a history of hiring ex-offenders to take leadership roles within his organizations and his ministry. "How can I not do that? They understand the cost of making life-changing mistakes, and the courage to get back on track. It is their way of paying it forward," says Tom.

The great ones are driven by something bigger than themselves. Business writer Jim Collins recently framed it perfectly when he stated that "most of the great leaders had the idea of *shaping the world around them*."[7] Business is much more than the production, distribution, and marketing of goods. Business is also about creating value with and for people. It is about leaving an imprint, and it is never easy. Leadership is about being human.

The best dark horse companies practice grace, and they

» HONOR OTHERS FOR WHO THEY ARE AND FOCUS ON THE GIFTS OF THE PERSON.
» INTENTIONALLY ATTRACT OTHER GREAT LEADERS TO JOIN THEIR ORGANIZATIONS.
» ARE NOT AFRAID OF CREATING A TEAM OF OTHER STRONG LEADERS.
» DO NOT CONTROL OTHERS' BEHAVIOR; ENCOURAGE OTHERS TO CREATE ON THEIR OWN TERMS.
» NEVER PUNISH OTHERS, BUT ALLOW OTHERS TO FEEL CONSEQUENCES OF BAD DECISIONS.
» DEMAND THE BEST, BUT DON'T WEIGH OTHERS DOWN WITH THE UNACHIEVABLE AND DEMORALIZING GOAL OF PERFECTION.
» UNDERSTAND THE IMPORTANCE OF CALLING OUT THE GOLD (THE BEST) IN MEMBERS OF THE TEAM.

Max De Pree once asked his Herman Miller leadership team a simple yet perplexing question: "*What should grace enable us to be?*" I have personally reflected on that question for over twenty years, and I have never heard a leader ask something so intimate and important. Great organizations (the best) understand the importance of pondering this idea.

During the final editing of this book, I had the chance to talk with Max De Pree on how leadership, grace, and business all fit together. De Pree wrote what some consider the most important book on leadership ever penned. It is not long, stuffy, highbrow, or complicated. It is filled with words like tears, love, covenant, and service. Max De Pree is now 89 years of age—and he took my phone call and invited me to talk with him in his office about grace, honor, and business. After watching what goes down in Washington and in most organizations, we are short on honor, calling, and authenticity. Max De Pree reminds us about the future of leadership and great organizations:

"A future leader has consistent and dependable integrity, cherishes diversity, searches out competence, is open to contrary opinion, communicates on all levels, understands and advocates for equity, is vulnerable to others, is intimate with others, is a spokesman and diplomat, is a tribal story teller, and tells why rather than how." [8]

The vision of leadership is not to attract followers; it's to create healthy, purposeful leaders who follow their individual identities.

Are we willing and courageous enough to live and work in a state of grace?

INSIGHTS ON GRACE

» GREAT ORGANIZATIONS AND LEADERS COME IN ALL STYLES, BUT THE RIGHT BAL-ANCE OF TRUTH AND GRACE UNLOCKS ORGANIZATIONAL SUCCESS.

» BUSINESS, LIKE LIFE, IS ABOUT MANAGING PARADOX WHILE MAINTAINING YOUR PEACE.

» REAL LEADERSHIP IS THE ART OF BEING *ALL IN* WITH YOUR VISION BUT HOLDING IT WITH AN OPEN PALM.

» DIVERSE HIRING PRACTICES ALLOWS FOR UNIQUE EXPRESSION, WHICH UNLEASHES INNOVATION AND AUTHENTICITY.

» ENCOURAGE DISSENT; SEEK CRITICAL FEEDBACK. IT TAKES GUTS TO SURROUND YOURSELF WITH ADVISORS WHO MAKE YOU A LITTLE UNEASY, KNOW MORE THAN YOU, AND ARE BLUNT.

» DARK HORSES ARE ADEPT AT UNLEASHING THE GOLD BURIED WITHIN THE MEMBERS OF THEIR TEAM. LEADERS THAT EXTEND GRACE ARE TRANSFORMATIONAL LEADERS.

» GRACE CREATES AN ATMOSPHERE OF TRUST. IT CANNOT BE REGULATED, AND MUST BE CAUGHT AND NOT BOUGHT.

THOUGHT STARTERS

1. HAVE YOU ASKED EACH MEMBER OF YOUR TEAM HOW YOU CAN ASSIST THEM IN ACHIEVING *THEIR* LIFE GOALS?

2. ARE YOU CULTIVATING TRUST RATHER THAN CONTROL IN YOUR TEAM?

3. HOW IS YOUR ORGANIZATION AT ATTRACTING AND RETAINING INDIVIDUALS WITH THEIR OWN STRONG IDEAS?

4. WHAT IS GETTING IN THE WAY OF UNLEASHING AND RETAINING YOUR TOP TALENT?

5. IS YOUR COMPENSATION A STRONG BALANCE OF BASE AND CUSTOMER RELATIONSHIP-BASED COMPENSATION?

6. WHAT, OTHER THAN FINANCIAL INCENTIVES, MOTIVATES AND IMPROVES YOUR ORGANIZATION'S PERFORMANCE?

7. CAN YOU HANDLE THE TRUTH AS A LEADER, AND HOW DO YOU KNOW?

8. ARE YOU KNOWN FOR CALLING OUT THE GOLD IN YOUR ORGANIZATION, OR DO YOU UTILIZE CONTROL TO DRIVE PERFORMANCE?

1 *last thought*

Almost twenty-five years ago, I was both moved and changed by a little 148 page book written by the CEO of Zeeland Michigan's Herman Miller—recognized for decades as one of the most trusted and admired companies in the world. That author was Max De Pree, and his deeply personal insights on leadership, organizational effectiveness, and creating a corporate culture of honor influenced me as a young manager and an even younger leader. His words set a standard that still directs me today.

Over the last three years, I have researched and interviewed a number of high performing leaders that have created special organizations, and Max De Pree's leadership standard has been my lens to gauge corporate success. Making a great product is important, but creating a special company—one that inspires, innovates, and is the type of environment where you would want your kids to work—is what you'd call *unique*. Max De Pree understands the difference, having led Herman Miller to heights most leaders will never realize. Herman Miller designs beautiful products (office equipment, desks, chairs, etc.), but the culture is even more distinctive. Max De Pree helped create the culture of Herman Miller, which is consistently recognized as one of Fortune Magazine's "Most Admired Companies" and, per CNN Money (March 2011), is one of the most admired companies in the Home Equipment Furnishing division. Even today, more than twenty-five years after stepping out of the Chief Executive role, Max De Pree challenges one's view of leadership and the role of being a leader.

During a fall afternoon in Michigan, I asked Max to share with me insights that "matter" in creating a culture that nurtures and encourages healthy leadership, beautiful innovation, and the development of a new generation of leaders.

The following are five philosophies that came out of our discussion together:

1. Special leaders unite people around an exceptional cause, clearly communicate ideas, walk with integrity, and are accepting while demonstrating accessibility. They understand that work is natural, should be done well, and can be truly redemptive and healing.

2. Great leaders are not afraid of vulnerability. This comes easier with age, as one no longer has to always prove oneself or fight for position. Vulnerability allows approachability and real insight into how you are doing. Exceptional leaders create a low risk atmosphere for people to want to share their hearts and their concerns.

3. The role of a leader is not to know it all. The leader's role is to discover competence in others and then to trust them. When someone is better than them at something, healthy leaders hand it off, because they no longer have the right to do it anymore. It is now meant for someone else, and one must learn to let go of things, even if they love doing them.

4. Leadership is very different than management. Leadership is not about answers; it is about asking the right questions. These are the questions that stay with others for years, the ones that are pondered the rest of one's life. Great questions elicit responses, but it's not about the response—it's whether the question stays with a person and transforms him.

5. Leadership is about serving others. It is about supporting others and truly getting to know the inspirations of others. One must be able to answer the question, "Who do we have working here?" It's about understanding an individual's identity, loves, dreams, and their essence, and it is only achieved through deep listening.

As I sat in Max's office overlooking Lake Macatawa, he reminded me of a story that he shared in his writings. The story goes as such: when his father was early in his career, a member of the company died, and Max's father went to the home to visit the wife of his employee. The man who had passed away was the millwright in the organization. The millwright was the person who came into the factory early in the morning to set up and start the machines while also maintaining the mechanical equipment. At the wake, the millwright's wife shared a touching poem that her husband had written. In fact, he had written numerous beautiful pieces; he was, indeed, a poet. Years later, Max and his father pondered the question, "Was he a millwright who was a poet, or a poet who was a millwright?" Leaders need to deeply know members of the team as people, parents, artists, and as sons and daughters in order to truly lead them. If this much is true, we have to create a trusting atmosphere where respect and love is the norm, while assisting everyone to unleash their individual gifts.

Creating a culture of honor and offering grace is part of the game of leadership.

ACTI

ON
MATTERS

Take time to deliberate; but when the time for action arrives, stop thinking and go in.

—NAPOLEON BONAPARTE

If you have made it to this part of the book, we are kindred souls. You are not satisfied with where you are at; you are an idea person, and you are more than likely always looking for an edge.

At last count, there are more than 200 ideas in this book that the best have shared with me on creating their winning organizations. These clues are significant if you take the time and incorporate them into your philosophy and operations.

The best are always looking for clues. Any kind of clues.

Recently I heard Robert Plant, the former lead vocalist of Led Zeppelin, say that he was hanging out in Austin, Texas, "looking for clues"—ideas and truths to inspire him in his art. If you are a music zealot like me, you recognize that Robert Plant was the voice of a decade, and one of the great musical innovators of the past forty years. He has the edge, yet he is as hungry as a new artist trying to find his path.

Robert Plant understands that there are clues all around us; they might be hidden, but they are calling out to us all.

This book is not a blueprint, but a way to help you ask very different questions about yourself and how you use your craft to create value while potentially making a difference in a way that *only you can.*

The ideas shared in this book offer an edge, if you look deeply at yourself and if you act upon them. The ten clues include:

1. Are you truly distinct in your calling and identity?

2. Do your customers understand your value, and do you understand your customers?

3. Are you inspired by your company mission and your role in changing the world?

4. Do you ask others on your team what unique assets you are not utilizing?

5. Do you get excited creating solution with your customers

6. Do you thrive in messiness and do you encourage an agile/ flexible culture?

7. Are you playing on the fringe, looking for where the ball is going, not where it is today?

8. Do you have a one-page strategic blueprint that is a working, breathing document that directs your course?

9. Do you have a group of believers who also serve as influencers for your cause?

10. Do you speak truth and extend grace to your organization?

We all cheer for the underdog because we see ourselves in their eyes. We admire them, root for them, and trust in their rise to fame.

Dark horses come from behind, even against seemingly insurmountable odds. And they win the race anyway.

Every day, another dark horse sneaks around the corner looking to steal the day. It is not by chance that they seize the moment. They are purposeful and practiced at their craft. And they believe in their rise to fame when others cannot imagine or conceive of their success.

The ten ideas outlined in this book are the top characteristics of distinct dark horse organizations who have overcome the odds. Take the time to ponder, reflect, discuss, and *act* on the ideas outlined in the book. We are all dark horses and your moment is *now*!

Bibliography

Bennis, Warren. *On Becoming a Leader.* Addison-Wesley, 1989.

Bradbury, Ray. "Management From Within." *New Management* Vol. I, No.4, 1984.

Champy, Jim. *Outsmart! How To Do What Your Competitors Can't.* FT Press, 2008.

Cialdini, Robert. *Influence: The Psychology of Persuasion.* Harper Collins Publishers, 1988.

Clancy, Kevin J., and Robert S. Shulman. *The Marketing Revolution: A Radical Manifesto for Dominating the Marketplace.* New York: HarperCollins, 1991.

Collins, Jim. *Good to Great.* Harper Collins Publishers, 2001.

Crawford, Fred, and Ryan Mathews. *The Myth of Excellence: Why Great Companies Never Try to Be the Best at Everything.* Crown Business, 2001.

Crum, Thomas. *The Magic of Conflict: Turning a Life of Work into a Work of Art.* Touchstone, 1987.

D'Aveni, Richard A., with Robert Gunther. *Hypercompetition: Managing the Dynamics of Strategic Maneuvering.* New York: The Free Press, 1994.

De Pree, Max. *Leadership is an Art.* Dell Publishing, 1989.

De Pree, Max. *Leadership Jazz.* Currency Doubleday, 1992.

Dru, Jean-Marie. *Disruption: Overturning Conventions and Shaking Up the Marketplace.* John Wiley & Sons, 1996.

Fisher, Roger, and William Ury. *Getting to Yes: Negotiating Agreement Without Giving In.* Penguin, 1981.

Bennis, Warren. *On Becoming a Leader.* Addison-Wesley, 1989.

Bradbury, Ray. "Management From Within." *New Management* Vol. I, No.4, 1984.

Champy, Jim. *Outsmart! How To Do What Your Competitors Can't.* FT Press, 2008.

Cialdini, Robert. *Influence: The Psychology of Persuasion.* Harper Collins Publishers, 1988.

Clancy, Kevin J., and Robert S. Shulman. *The Marketing Revolution: A Radical Manifesto for Dominating the Marketplace.* New York: HarperCollins, 1991.

Collins, Jim. *Good to Great.* Harper Collins Publishers, 2001.

Crawford, Fred, and Ryan Mathews. *The Myth of Excellence: Why Great Companies Never Try to Be the Best at Everything.* Crown Business, 2001.

Crum, Thomas. *The Magic of Conflict: Turning a Life of Work into a Work of Art.* Touchstone, 1987.

D'Aveni, Richard A., with Robert Gunther. *Hypercompetition: Managing the Dynamics of Strategic Maneuvering.* New York: The Free Press, 1994.

De Pree, Max. *Leadership is an Art.* Dell Publishing, 1989.

De Pree, Max. *Leadership Jazz.* Currency Doubleday, 1992.

Dru, Jean-Marie. *Disruption: Overturning Conventions and Shaking Up the Marketplace.* John Wiley & Sons, 1996.

Fisher, Roger, and William Ury. *Getting to Yes: Negotiating Agreement Without Giving In.* Penguin, 1981.

Gladwell, Malcolm. *The Tipping Point: How Little Things Can Make a Big Difference.* Little, Brown and Company, 2000.

Gobé, Marc. *Emotional Branding: The New Paradigm for Connecting Brands to People.* Allworth Press, 2001.

Handy, Charles. *The Age of Paradox.* Harvest Business School Press, 1994.

Handy, Charles. *The Age of Unreason.* Boston: Harvard Business School Press, 1990.

Horwath, Rich. *Deep Dive: The Proven Method for Building Strategy, Focusing Your Resources, and Taking Smart Action.* Greenleaf Book Group, 2009.

Kriegel, Robert J., and Louis Patler. *If It Ain't Broke... Break It!* New York: Warner Brooks, 1991.

Lamott, Anne. *Traveling Mercies.* Anchor Books, 1999.

Levitt, Theodore. *The Marketing Imagination.* The Free Press, 1986.

McKenna, Regis. *Real Time: Preparing for the Age of the Never Satisfied Customer.* Harvard Business School Press, 1997.

McKenna, Regis. *Relationship Marketing: Successful Strategies for the Age of the Consumer.* Addison-Wesley, 1991.

Moon, Youngme. *Different: Escaping the Competitive Herd.* Crown Business, 2010.

Morgan, Adam. *Eating the Big Fish: How Challenger Brands Can*

Compete Against Brand Leaders. John Wiley & Sons, 1999.

Pascale, Richard T., Mark Millemann, and Linda Gioja. *Surfing the Edge of Chaos: The Laws of Nature and the New Laws of Business.* Crown Business, 2000.

Patterson, Kerry, Joseph Grenny, David Maxfield, Ron McMillan, and Al Switzler. *Influencer: The Power to Change Anything.* McGraw-Hill, 2008.

Peters, Tom. *Re-imagine! Business Excellence in a Disruptive Age.* DK Publishing, 2003.

Peters, Tom. *The Circle of Innovation.* Alfred A. Knopf, 1997.

Peters, Tom. *The Pursuit of Wow! Every Person's Guide to Topsy-Turvy Times.* London: Pan Books, 1993.

Peters, Tom. *The Tom Peters Seminar: Crazy Times Call for Crazy Organizations.* London: Pan Books, 1994.

Peters, Tom. *Thriving on Chaos: Handbook for a Management Revolution.* Alfred A. Knopf Inc., 1987.

Popcorn, Faith, and Lys Marigold. *EVEolution: The Eight Truths of Marketing to Women.* Hyperion, 2000.

Rackham, Neil. "The New Selling: From Communicating Value to Creating Value." In *Rethinking the Sales Force*, 8–9. McGraw-Hill, 1999.

Rackham, Neil. *Major Account Sales Strategy.* McGraw-Hill, 1989.

Rapp, Stan, and Tom Collins. *MaxiMarketing: The New Direction in Advertising, Promotion, and Marketing Strategy.* New York: McGraw-Hill, 1987.

Ray, Michael, and Rochelle Myers. *Creativity in Business.* Bantam Doubleday Dell, 1986.

Ridderstråle, Jonas, and Kjell Nordström. *Funky Business Forever.* Bookhouse Publishing, 2000.

Ries, Al, and Jack Trout. *Positioning: The Battle for Your Mind.* New York: Warner Books, 1986.

Rowley, Laura. *On Target: How the World's Hottest Retailer Hit a Bull's-Eye.* John Wiley & Sons, 2003.

Schembechler, Bo, and John Bacon. *Bo's Lasting Lessons.* Hachett Book Group, 2007.

Senge, Peter M. *The Fifth Discipline: The Art and Practice of the Learning Organization.* Bantam Doubleday Dell Publishing Group, 1990.

Slater, Robert. *The Wal-Mart Decade.* Penguin Group, 2003.

Slywotzky, Adrian. *The Art of Profitability.* Warner Books, 2002.

Slywotzky, Adrian. *Value Migration: How to Think Several Moves Ahead of the Competition.* Corporate Decisions Inc., 1996.

Stockman, Steve. *Walk On: The Spiritual Journey of U2.* Relevant Books, 2005.

Underhill, Paco. *Why We Buy: The Science of Shopping.* Touchstone, 1999.

REFERENCES AND SOURCES

INTRODUCTION: WHAT IS A "DARK HORSE" ANYWAY?

From December 2008 to December 2012 I interviewed many of the top merchandising and buying executives (current and past) from Walgreens, CVS, Rite Aid, Ulta Beauty, Wal-Mart, Costco, Sam's Club, and other buying influencers. This research has helped frame much of the content in this book and my current consulting practice.

CHAPTER 1: IDENTITY

[1] Max De Pree, *Leadership is an Art* (Dell Publishing, 1989).

[2] My thinking on Bruce Springsteen was a paraphrase of a comment he voiced back in the late 1970s at the peak of his innovative writing.

[3] Chris Arnold, "Wiffle Ball: Born and Still Made in the USA," NPR.org, September 5, 2011, http://www.npr.org/2011/09/05/140145711/wiffle-ball-born-and-still-made-in-the-usa.

[4] David Mielach, "After 60 years, Wiffle Ball Still Soars," BusinessNewsDaily.com, April 28, 2012, http://www.businessnewsdaily.com/2430-wiffle-ball-maker-story.html.

[5] Greg Wahl (President and CEO of Wahl Home Products), in discussion with author.

[6] Blair Kellison (CEO, Traditional Medicinals) and Darrick Blinoff (VP of Sales, Traditional Medicinals), in discussion with author. Also, http://www.traditionalmedicinals.com/.

[7] Eric Ryan, in discussion with author. Also, http://methodhome.com/.

[8] Whole Foods website, http://www.wholefoodsmarket.com/whole-foods-market.

[9] Max Nisen, "Whole Foods Founder Says Too Many Companies Get Capitalism Wrong," BusinessInsider.com, January 17, 2013, http://www.businessinsider.com/whole-foods-ceo-on-reclaiming-capitalism-2013-1.

CHAPTER 2: ALIGNMENT

[1] Paul Leinwand and Cesare R. Mainardi, "Executives Say They're Pulled in Too Many Directions and That Their Company's Capabilities Don't Support Their Strategy," Booz & Company website, January 18, 2011, http://www.booz.com/global/home/press/article/49007867.

[2] Charles Wachsberg (CEO, Apollo Health and Beauty Care), in discussion with author.

[3] Dan Richard (National Sales Manager, NOW Foods), in discussion with author. Also, summation from the NOW Foods wholesaler catalog (September–December 2011), 34.

[4] Kelly Kaplan (President and COO, Revive Personal Products), in discussion with author. Also, Revive website, http://www.revivepersonalproducts.com/.

[5] Bill Higgins (President, Ricola U.S.), in discussion with author about the strategy and culture of Ricola. Also http://www.ricola.com/en-ch.

[6] Bill Graham (President, General Manager Beiersdorf North America), in discussion with the author.

[7] Justin Menkes, "Three Traits Every CEO Needs," Harvard Business Review—HBR Blog Network, May 11, 2011, http://blogs.hbr.org/cs/2011/05/three_traits_every_ceo_needs.html.

CHAPTER 3: HIDDEN ASSETS

[1] *The Economist*, 1996.

[2] Robert Cialdini, *Influence: The Psychology of Persuasion* (Harper Collins Publishers, 1988), 110.

[3] Joe Kanfer (CEO of GOJO Industries) in discussion with author.

[4] Youngme Moon, *Different: Escaping the Competitive Herd* (Crown Business, 2010), 7–8.

[5] Moon, *Different: Escaping the Competitive Herd*, 11–12.

[6] Moon, *Different: Escaping the Competitive Herd*, 12–13, 37.

[7] Ido Leffler (co-founder and leader of Yes To Inc.) in discussion with author.

[8] Author's DenTek field interviews, internal discussion, and personal observations while working for the organization as the leader of sales.

CHAPTER 4: THE VITAL FEW

[1] Josh Hyatt, "Playing Favorites," *CEO Magazine* (2010).

[2] Sandra M. Jones, "Meijer Moves in on Chicago," *Chicago Tribune*, August 28, 2011.

[3] Mike Pietsch (VP of Sales and Marketing, Carma Labs), in discussion with author.

[4] Eric Ryan (co-founder of Method Inc.) and George Shumny (VP of Sales during the high-growth years) in interview.

CHAPTER 5: CO-CREATION

[1] *My Starbucks Idea*, http://www.starbucks.ca/coffeehouse/learn-more/my-starbucks-idea.

[2] My thinking in this area was greatly influenced by Neil Rackham's "The New Selling: From Communicating Value to Creating Value" in *Rethinking the Sales Force: Redefining Selling to Create and Capture Customer Value,* (McGraw-Hill, 1999), 8–9.

[3] My thinking in this area were reflections during my time leading the sales process with GOJO Industries from 1999–2005.

[4] Lex Shankle (former VP of Marketing, DenTek Oral Care), in discussion with author.

[5] Ido Leffler (co-founder and leader of Yes To Inc.), in discussion with author.

[6] Insights come from multiple interviews with Charles Wachsberg (CEO of Apollo).

[7] The Sunset Foods case study is sourced through my own personal patronage of the establishment, with marketing insights taken from their web site, http://www.sunsetfoods.com/.

CHAPTER 6: THE BLUEPRINT

[1] Kerry Patterson, et al., *Influencer: The Power to Change Anything* (McGraw-Hill, 2008), 159.

[2] Rich Horwath, *Deep Dive: The Proven Method for Building Strategy, Focusing Your Resources, and Taking Smart Action* (Greenleaf Book Group, 2009).

[3] Kerry Patterson, et al., *Influencer: The Power to Change Anything* (McGraw-Hill, 2008), 159.

[4] U2, *How to Dismantle an Atomic Bomb* (2004). Inspired by Bono's comments on the making of the new CD.

[5] Bo Schembechler and John Bacon, *Bo's Lasting Lessons* (Hachett Book Group, 2007).

[6] Bruce Kramer (VP of Sales and Marketing, Wahl), in interview with author.

[7] Bill Graham (President, General Manager Beiersdorf North America), in interview with author.

[8] Bill Higgins (President of Ricola U.S.) in interview with author.

CHAPTER 7: INFLUENCERS

[1] Kerry Patterson, et al., *Influencer: The Power to Change Anything* (McGraw-Hill, 2008), 50.

[2] Patterson, et al., *Influencer: The Power to Change Anything*, 148.

[3] Patterson, et al., *Influencer: The Power to Change Anything*, 153.

[4] Patterson, et al., *Influencer: The Power to Change Anything*, 51.

[5] Amy's Kitchen at http://www.amys.com/.

[6] Derma E skin care products at http://www.dermae.com/.

[7] Stonyfield Yogurt web site http://www.stonyfield.com/, and a compilation of retailer interviews, field assessments, and a whole bunch of personal yogurt consumption.

[8] Jen Boynton, "Scaling Stonyfield Yogurt," TriplePundit.com, April 18, 2012, http://www.triplepundit.com/2012/04/economics-stonyfield-yogurt/.

[9] Marc Gobé, *Emotional Branding: The New Paradigm for Connecting Brands to People* (Allworth Press, 2001). Summation was inspired by xxviii–xxxi.

[10] Patterson, et al., *Influencer: The Power to Change Anything*, 59–61.

[11] Jonas Ridderstråle and Kjell Nordström, *Funky Business Forever* (Bookhouse Publishing, 2000), 78, 83.

[12] Kerry Fehr-Snyder, "Herbal Cold Remedy Goes Airborne after Oprah Plug," *Arizona Republic*, January 29, 2005.

[13] Mike Pietsch (VP of Sales and Marketing for Carma Labs), in interview with author.

CHAPTER 8: AGILITY

[1] Richard T. Pascale, Mark Millemann, and Linda Gioja, *Surfing the Edge of Chaos: The Laws of Nature and the New Laws of Business* (Crown Business, 2000), 6.

[2] Dan Richard (National Sales Manager of NOW Foods), in interview with author.

[3] Insights from a discussion with two former DenTek Oral Care executives.

[4] Richard A. D'Aveni with Robert Gunther, *Hypercompetition: Managing the Dynamics of Strategic Maneuvering* (New York: The Free Press, 1994), 10, 30–31.

[5] Paco Underhill, *Why We Buy: The Science of Shopping* (Touchstone, 1999), 163.

[6] Interviews with Apollo's Chief Executive Charles Wachsberg.

[7] Underhill, *Why We Buy: The Science of Shopping*, 166.

[8] John Tozzi, "Think Twice About Being First to Market," *Bloomberg Business Week*, May 19, 2009, http://www.businessweek.com/smallbiz/content/may2009/sb20090519_306313.htm.

[9] Youngme Moon, *Different: Escaping the Competitive Herd* (Crown Publishing Group, 2010), 7, 12.

[10] Ido Leffler (co-founder and leader of Yes To Inc.), in interview with author.

CHAPTER 9: SURF THE SOCIETAL SHIFTS
[1] Marc Gobé, Emotional Branding: The New Paradigm for Connecting Brands to People (Allworth Press, 2001), xxii.

[682] Jupiter Media Metrix (July 20, 2001). Global Napster Usage Plummets, But New File-Sharing Alternatives Gaining Ground. Press Release.

[3] *Reinvigorated Bottled Water Bounces Back from Recessionary Years, New Report From Beverage Marketing Corporation Shows*, BeverageMarketing.com press release, Beverage Marketing Company of New York, May 2012, http://www.beveragemarketing.com/index.asp?section=pressreleases.

[4] Scott Pakula (sales leader for EOS) in interview with author.

[5] Joe Kanfer (CEO of GOJO Industries), in interview with author.

[6] "Small Business: Joe Coffee Brewing in NYC," Nightly Business Report, June 14, 2012.

CHAPTER 10: A CULTURE OF GRACE
[1] Tamara Schweitzer, "The Way I Work: Blake Mycoskie of Toms Shoes," *Inc. Magazine*, June 1, 2010, http://www.inc.com/magazine/20100601/the-way-i-work-blake-mycoskie-of-toms-shoes.html.

[2] Charles Handy, *The Age of Paradox* (Harvest Business School Press, 1994), 47.

[3] Handy, *The Age of Paradox*, 48.

[4] Blair Kellison (President of Traditional Medicinals), in interview with author.

[5] Gary Hamel, Keynote Address in West Palm Beach Florida, NACDS, April 2011.

[6] Warren Bennis, *On Becoming a Leader* (Addison-Wesley, 1989). Bennis's book is a model for a number of the top-run companies.

[7] Bo Burlingham, "Jim Collins: Be Great Now," *Inc. Magazine*, May 2012, http://www.inc.com/magazine/201206/bo-burlingham/jim-collins-exclusive-interview-be-great-now.html.

[8] Max De Pree, *Leadership is an Art* (Dell Publishing, 1989). 120, 131

ACKNOWLEDGEMENTS

Thank you to Heather Angus-Lee, Peter Santilli, and Evan Mack for your editorial wisdom. You three brought order out of a group of ideas.

To Rania Meng for your creative support on the design of the book.

And to Derek Vasconi for your fierce passion and love of art.

ABOUT THE AUTHOR

Dan Mack brings twenty-five years of strategic sales, business development, and national industry insights to his clients. Dan is founder of Mack Elevation Forum, a strategic sales practice that provides alignment and growth consulting to health and wellness organizations.

Dan Mack served as the Vice President of Sales & Customer Marketing at DenTek Oral Care, a manufacturer of specialty oral care items. Mack was responsible for leading the customer strategy, and sales more than doubled during Mack's tenure.

Prior to DenTek, Mack was the V.P. of Consumer Sales at GOJO Industries. While at GOJO, he developed and led a national sales organization which helped grow the PURELL consumer business almost four-fold over his seven-year tenure.

Mack started his career with GlaxoSmithKline and held many leadership roles including National Manager of Sales Training and Divisional Sales Manager.

Dan has led a number of led key note addresses in the package goods industry and contributes editorials on sales strategy, organizational effectiveness, customer alignment, and executive training. His industry specialization is in helping companies facilitate higher-level retailer/supplier co-creation engagements and is a specialist in value creation.

He lives in Chicago with his wife and family.

DAN
MACK

Made in the USA
Middletown, DE
27 February 2017